play like

Audio Access Included!

Elton John

The Ultimate Piano Lesson

T0047472

by Mark Harrison

To access audio visit:
www.halleonard.com/mylibrary

Enter Code
3898-7101-9467-5255

Cover photo: KMazur/ WireImage/Getty Images

ISBN 978-1-4803-9198-7

HAL•LEONARD®
CORPORATION
7777 W. BLUEMOUND RD. P.O. BOX 13819 MILWAUKEE, WI 53213

Copyright © 2015 by HAL LEONARD CORPORATION
International Copyright Secured   All Rights Reserved

For all works contained herein:
Unauthorized copying, arranging, adapting, recording, Internet posting, public performance,
or other distribution of the printed or recorded music in this publication is an infringement of copyright
Infringers are liable under the law.

Visit Hal Leonard Online at
www.halleonard.com

CONTENTS

INTRODUCTION

Welcome to *Play Like Elton John*, the ultimate guide to learning how to play like its eponymous pop icon. Elton John has exerted a huge influence on the development of popular music during a career spanning over 50 years. We'll take a close look at some of Elton's most famous songs and dissect his trademark harmonic and rhythmic techniques, which have influenced generations of piano and keyboard players.

This book is organized into several sections, each focusing on different aspects of Elton John's music and career:

Equipment

Although Elton has mainly been associated with the acoustic grand piano throughout his career, he has also made use of digital pianos and synthesizers. Here, we highlight some of his equipment history and the instruments used.

Songs

Here we'll take a detailed look at transcriptions of five of Elton's most classic and enduring songs. We'll closely study Elton's specific piano techniques, and how he achieves his trademark sound. Each song will have a complete audio recording with a full band track, as well as accompanying lessons focusing on specific sections of the song.

Signature Phrases

Here we'll take a close look at some signature parts, exactly as they were played by Elton John, on ten more of his most famous songs. Each signature phrase is demonstrated on the audio, together with accompanying band tracks for each.

Integral Techniques

Here we'll explore some of the playing techniques and rhythmic tricks that will enable you to get inside Elton's playing style. Each integral technique is demonstrated with three audio examples, including accompanying band tracks.

Stylistic DNA

Here we'll delve into the structural components of Elton's signature piano style, including some of his favorite harmonic and melodic devices. Each stylistic DNA point is demonstrated with three audio examples, including accompanying band tracks.

Must Hear

Here we'll spotlight the essential albums and songs that Elton has written and recorded over his long, illustrious career.

Must See

This focuses on some important video highlights of Elton's live performances, both on DVD and on YouTube.

ABOUT THE AUDIO

To access the audio examples that accompany this book, simply go to **www.halleonard.com/mylibrary** and enter the code found on the title page. This will grant you instant access to every example. Throughout the book, the examples that include audio are marked with an audio icon. The audio tracks relating to the "Excerpts from Full Songs" have the right-hand part on the right channel and the left-hand part on the left channel. The other audio tracks (Signature Phrases, Integral Techniques, Stylistic DNA) have the backing band on the left channel and the piano part (hands together) on the right channel. The full song demo tracks include both the piano part and the backing band.

EQUIPMENT

During Elton's early career, he mainly used Steinway grand pianos, most often the Model D concert grand, revered among classical and pop musicians alike. However, in the mid-1980s he began incorporating the Roland RD1000 digital piano into his live setup. The RD1000 is a "modeled" rather than "sampled" digital piano; in other words, the piano sound is generated digitally, instead of triggering a recording (or "sample") of a real piano. The RD1000 has a bright, expressive sound that Elton liked, although it is considered less "realistic" when strictly compared to the sound of a grand piano.

Then in the early 1990s Elton abruptly ended his relationship with Steinway, when he decided shortly before a concert that the Steinway piano just didn't cut through the band sound when playing live. For the performance, a Yamaha CFIII concert grand was hurriedly obtained from a college near the venue. Elton has used Yamaha grand pianos in studios and onstage ever since, and currently has five Yamaha nine-foot-long grand pianos in various locations worldwide. He names each of these pianos after famous female jazz singers/performers, such as Aretha (Franklin), Diana (Krall), and Nina (Simone).

One of Elton's most celebrated instruments is the Million Dollar Piano, a grand piano made for him by Yamaha for his resident show at Caesar's Palace in Las Vegas, beginning in 2011. This custom Yamaha grand took four years to complete, and has a glass top, LED lights around the side panels, and over 60 video screens displaying various images during the concert performance. In keeping with his tradition of naming pianos after female artists, this extravagant instrument is nicknamed "Blossom," after the late jazz singer/pianist Blossom Dearie. Elton's performance on this piano at Caesar's Palace is documented on the best-selling *Million Dollar Piano* live DVD, released in 2014.

In recent years, while Elton's onstage Yamaha pianos are fully functioning instruments, all of the "front-of-house" (i.e., what the audience hears) and monitor sounds are digital. The Yamaha pianos are retrofitted as MIDI controllers, and they enable Elton to trigger various sound modules from the acoustic piano keyboard. These modules include the Roland MKS-20 (a rack version of the RD1000 digital piano mentioned above), as well as the Yamaha Motif XS rack module (which contains various electric piano and string sounds, among others). This allows Elton to change sounds from song to song as needed, while still playing everything from the acoustic piano keyboard.

Another reason Elton prefers to use these electronic sounds is that he doesn't like to use in-ear monitors, and he prefers his onstage monitoring level to be very loud – around 120dB. At that level, it can be impractical to "mic up" an acoustic piano without drastic equalization (tone-shaping) to avoid feedback. The use of purely electronic sounds solves this problem, although some might say this comes at the expense of piano realism (i.e., sounding precisely like an acoustic grand piano).

Elton has also used modern digital technology to share his performances in interesting ways. For example, at a concert at the 2013 NAMM show in Anaheim CA, he performed on a Yamaha Disklavier, which is able to record and play back performances using a type of "digital piano roll" technology. Since 2010, these instruments have also had a remote operation feature enabling a Disklavier-equipped piano to "play" another in real time. So Elton John fans (and Disklavier owners) worldwide were able to stream the data from this concert into their homes, and see their piano keys and pedals move in sync with his performance!

SONGS

In this section of the book, we'll look at complete transcriptions for five of Elton John's most famous songs. From these, we'll then take five piano excerpts from each one, exactly as Elton played them on the recordings, and use them as a basis for an in-depth lesson. We'll explore his harmonic, rhythmic, and stylistic choices for each example in detail, all of which will enable you to get inside his trademark sound as quickly as possible.

Don't Let the Sun Go Down on Me
(*Caribou*, 1974)

Elton wrote this song together with lyricist Bernie Taupin in January 1974; it was the first single released from the *Caribou* album later that year. One of his most classic and enduring ballads, the song also shows Elton's gospel piano influences. The song had its greatest success when later released as a duet with George Michael in 1991, reaching No. 1 in both the U.K. and the U.S. The song has also been covered by various other artists, including Gloria Estefan, Joe Cocker, and the Winans.

Now we'll take a look at the song section by section. For your reference, the song transcription begins on page 9.

Intro

The Intro to this song is a good place for us to meet some signature Elton John piano techniques used throughout this book:

Right Hand
- Extensive use of major and minor triads and arpeggios, often with octave doubling (top note of the triad doubled one octave lower)
- Use of voice leading between chords (moving closely between successive inversions)
- Use of resolutions within triads (moving from the 4th to the 3rd, or from the 9th to the root)
- Use of quarter-note, eighth-note, and 16th-note rhythmic subdivisions

Left Hand
- Normally the root of each chord is played as the bottom note, except when the chord is inverted over its 3rd, 5th, or 7th. (This is a common Elton device, as we'll see later on.)
- Frequent use of octave intervals and root-5th intervals on chords
- Use of quarter-note, eighth-note, and 16th-note rhythmic subdivisions, including rhythmic pickups into downbeats

Now we'll check out the first four measures of this classic piano intro:

Don't Let the Sun
Go Down on Me
Example 1

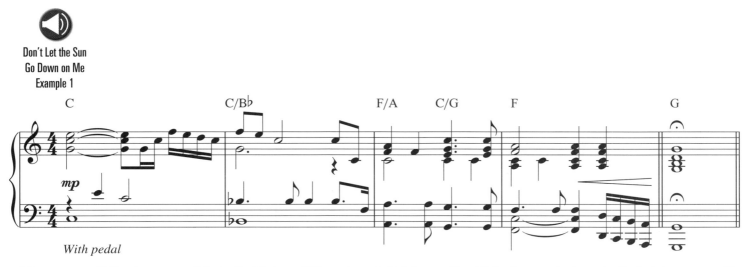

With pedal

Like many of Elton's songs, this ballad has a 16th-note subdivision or "feel." As for most piano ballad styles, you will need to depress the sustain pedal for the duration of each chord; be sure to release the pedal at the points of chord change.

The Intro starts with a simple C major triad in second inversion in the right hand, over the root of C in the left. Then halfway through beat 3 (or on the "& of 3") in the first measure, a 16th-note melodic line is created by combining two of the right-hand devices mentioned on page 5: an arpeggio (the C major triad played "broken-chord" style) together with a 4th-to-3rd resolution (the F moving to E at the start of beat 4). This resolution is then repeated, this time using eighth notes, at the start of the second measure.

A number of the chords are inverted over different notes in the bass: the C/B♭ chord in the second measure implies a C7 dominant chord inverted over its 7th, and the F/A and C/G chords in the third measure are major triads inverted over their 3rd and 5th respectively. All this creates a pleasing melodic line in the bass voice: C–B♭–A–G–F.

The left hand is landing on beats 1 and 3 of each measure, often with an eighth-note pickup before beat 3. This is a common pop-rock piano device that adds forward motion to the rhythmic groove. Later in the third and fourth measures, the right hand adds energy through the use of octave-doubled triads, followed by a descending 16th-note left-hand run in octaves at the end of the fourth measure. This in turn leads into the strong G major chord (with octaves in both hands) in the fifth measure.

Verse

The Verse section begins at a fairly low intensity, with right-hand triads and four-part chords, and some ornamentation and pickups. Let's spotlight the section starting on the ninth measure of the Verse, where the energy begins to pick up a little:

Don't Let the Sun
Go Down on Me
Example 2

Note that the right-hand part is initially shown in the bass clef as it starts out mostly below middle C, and would therefore require too many ledger lines if written in the treble clef.

The combined rhythm between the hands in the first two measures shown is a classic Elton John setting: a right-hand quarter-note pulse, with the left hand on beats 1 and 3 and adding eighth-note pickups as described earlier.

This right-hand part is varied during beat 4 of the first measure shown, with the C major triad landing on the second 16th of beat 4. This is a weak 16th not available within an eighth-note subdivision; it creates a dramatic and effective syncopation.

Harmonically, this C major triad is a passing chord between the preceding G and following G7 chords, and demonstrates a common Elton device: the movement from I to IV and back to I again, as a harmonic embellishment within a chord. This is sometimes referred to as "backcycling" and is a staple of gospel and rock piano styles – more about this later on.

Toward the end of the third measure shown, a descending eighth-note melodic run begins in the right hand. This starts out with another common Elton technique: the use of "filled-in octaves," octave intervals with one extra note in between (for example, the F–A–F and E–G–E voicings during beat 4). These are followed by octave-doubled triads later in the fourth measure shown, further building the energy level, before resolving to the F major chord in the fifth measure shown.

Note that the "8vb" below the bass clef toward the end of this example means that the left hand is to be transposed down an octave. This is done to avoid excessive ledger lines in the bass clef part. (Elton often uses these low notes in the left hand, again reflecting a gospel influence.)

Next we'll skip to a later section in the verse: the four measures immediately preceding the Chorus. This has sparser rhythms, but some interesting syncopations:

Don't Let the Sun
Go Down on Me
Example 3

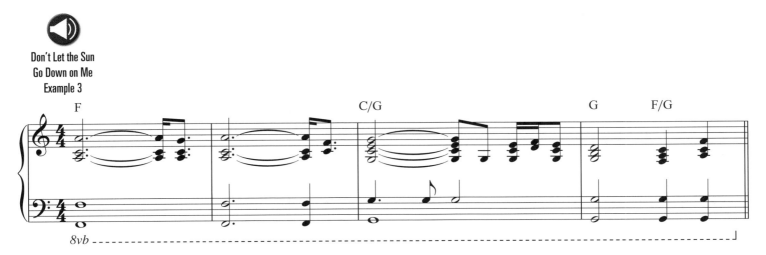

In the first two measures on the F major chord, we have a repeat of the filled-in octave approach in the right hand, with the A–C–A voicings. This gives good projection and power, but with less "density" than the octave-doubled triads seen earlier. The right hand also lands on the second 16th of beat 4 in these measures. As the only right-hand subdivision after beat 1 in these measures, this is a particularly noticeable syncopation.

Meanwhile, the left-hand root-note pattern gets busier in the third measure of this section (with an eighth-note pickup into beat 3), preceding the right-hand 16th-note fill based on the C major triad. Both hands then play "concerted" rhythms in the last measure before the chorus, with the right-hand triads supported by octaves in the left hand.

Harmony note: The F/G chord at the end of this section is an example of an "upper structure" triad voicing. The F major triad in the right hand is "built from" the 7th of the G suspended dominant chord, whose root is in the left hand. The notes in the upper F major triad are the 7th, 9th, and 11th of the overall chord. Alternate chord symbols you will see for this chord are G9sus or G11. This is a common Elton John voicing, and is used throughout pop and rock styles in general.

Chorus

In the full song transcription, the chorus section starts right after the end section of the verse we just looked at, and builds intensity with right-hand triads and rhythmic subdivisions, and left-hand octaves with pickups. Next we'll spotlight the section beginning in the seventh measure of the Chorus, where the energy builds further:

Don't Let the Sun
Go Down on Me
Example 4

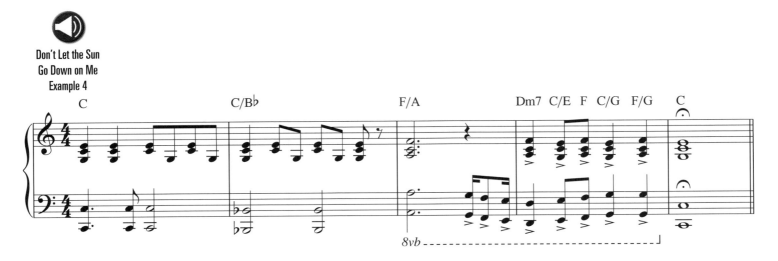

In the first two measures, the right hand is playing the C major triad either as quarter notes (at the start of these measures) or in an "alternating eighths" rock ballad style (during beats 3–4 in the first measure, and during beats 2–3 in the second measure).

"Alternating eighths" is a piano ballad accompaniment style in which the right hand plays all the triad tones except the lowest note, on the downbeat (i.e., beats 1, 2, 3, and/or 4), and then plays the lowest note of each triad on the following upbeat (i.e., on the "and of 1," "and of 2," and so on). Meanwhile, the left hand continues playing an octave pattern similar to the the first part of the chorus.

Then in the third measure of this section, there is an open area after the F/A chord played on beat 1, until the left-hand octave run beginning on beat 4. This run uses the second and fourth 16th-notes inside beat 4 (the "weak 16ths"), creating a strong syncopated effect.

In the fourth measure of this section, we see a much busier chord rhythm, with a combination of upper-structure triad voicings, and chords inverted over their 3rd or 5th in the bass. The Dm7 is voiced with an F major triad in the right hand, built from the 3rd of the overall Dm7 chord, whose root is in the left hand. The C/E and C/G chords, on either side of the F major chord, are C major triads inverted over their 3rd and 5th, respectively. The F/G is a voicing for a G suspended dominant chord, as we saw earlier in Example 3. Again, this series of voicings and inversions facilitates the ascending bass line of D–E–F–G in this measure; all are common Elton John harmonic choices.

In the full song transcription, we then continue to the next Verse section, after which we observe the *D.S. al Coda* instruction. This first takes us back to the Chorus, and then to the Coda, a short instrumental section before the final Chorus. Our next example spotlights the first four measures of this final Chorus section, which uses some different voicings and rhythmic subdivisions:

Don't Let the Sun
Go Down on Me
Example 5

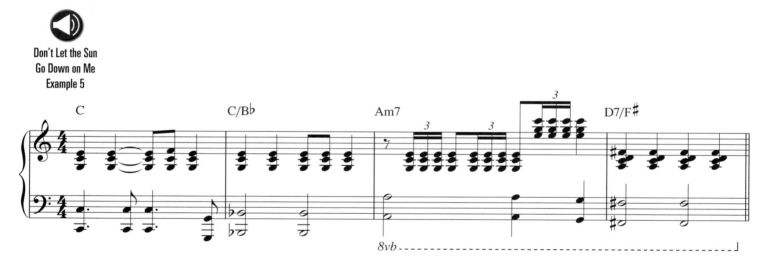

In the first two measures of this section on the C major chord, the right hand is based on a quarter-note pulse, with an eighth-note subdivision of beat 3. Note the 4th-to-3rd movement (F to E) inside the C major triad during the first measure, adding movement and melodic interest. Meanwhile, the left hand is playing in octaves on beats 1 and 3, with some eighth-note pickups as usual.

In the third measure of this section, Elton is again using an upper-structure triad voicing: building a C major triad in the right hand from the 3rd of the overall Am7 chord. This upper C major triad is also being played using 16th-note triplets, and in different inversions. All this is designed to increase the energy level and momentum at this point.

Then in the fourth measure on the D7/F♯ chord, the right hand reverts to a steady quarter-note pulse, using basic four-part dominant chords in second inversion. This is supported by simple half-note octaves in the left hand.

Again note the "8vb" written below the bass clef for the last two measures of this example. Make sure you play these left hand notes one octave lower than written.

DON'T LET THE SUN GO DOWN ON ME

Words and Music by Elton John and Bernie Taupin

Don't Let the Sun
Go Down on Me
Full Song

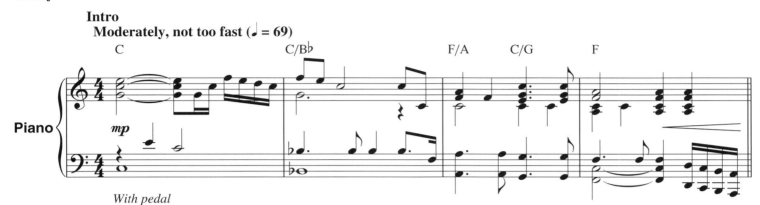

Copyright © 1974 HST MGT. LTD. and ROUGE BOOZE, INC.
Copyright Renewed
All Rights for HST MGT. LTD. in the United States and Canada Controlled and Administered by
UNIVERSAL - SONGS OF POLYGRAM INTERNATIONAL, INC.
All Rights for ROUGE BOOZE, INC. in the United States and Canada Controlled and Administered by
UNIVERSAL - POLYGRAM INTERNATIONAL PUBLISHING, INC.
All Rights Reserved   Used by Permission

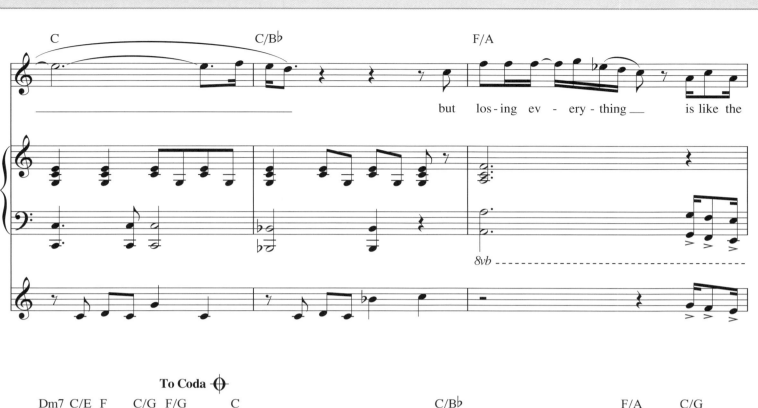

but los-ing ev-ery-thing __ is like the

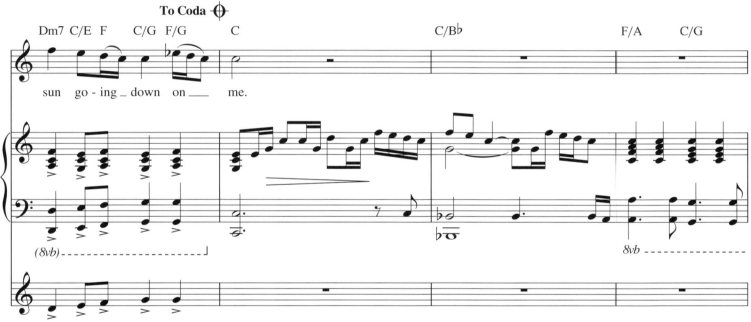

sun go-ing __ down on __ me.

I can't find __ oh, __ the right __ ro-

los - ing ev - ery - thing   is   like   the   sun   go - ing ___ down   on ___

me.

Rocket Man
(*Honky Chateau*, 1972)

"Rocket Man" was the first single released from Elton's 1972 *Honky Chateau* album. It became a hit on both sides of the Atlantic: No. 6 in the U.S. and No. 2 in the U.K. Another classic ballad written by Elton with lyricist Bernie Taupin, the song was inspired by a short story written by science fiction author Ray Bradbury. "Rocket Man" has been covered by many other artists, notably including a reggae-tinged version released by Kate Bush in 1991, which was a critical and commercial success.

Now we'll take a look at the song section by section. For your reference, the song transcription begins on page 23.

Verse

Unlike most Elton John songs, "Rocket Man" doesn't have an instrumental Intro section; it starts right away with the first vocal verse. This section begins with a mix of right-hand triads and four-part chords, using rhythmic punctuations rather than a steady pulse. Let's spotlight the section starting on the fifth measure of the Verse, where a quarter-note pulse starts to emerge:

Rocket Man
Example 1

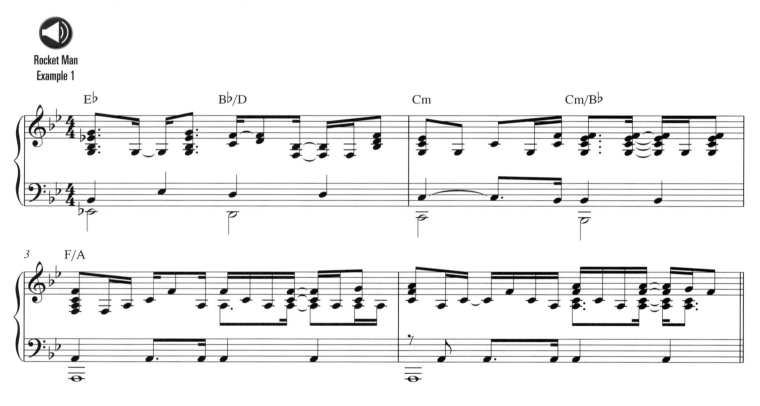

This ballad has a 16th-note subdivision or "feel." You will need to depress the sustain pedal for the duration of each chord.

This section demonstrates a classic Elton John rhythmic styling between the two hands. In the first measure shown, the left-hand pinky is playing the low chord roots on beats 1 and 3, with the thumb adding a quarter-note pulse above. The right hand is also landing on beats 1 and 3, and then mostly on the weak 16ths (the second and fourth 16th notes within each beat), including the 16th subdivisions on either side of beats 2 and 4 (the "backbeats").

In the third and fourth measures shown, the left-hand thumb adds 16th-note pickups into beat 3, and the right hand adds more arpeggios while still landing a 16th note ahead of beat 4 in these measures. All this combines to create a syncopated, R&B-influenced comping groove that is Elton's trademark.

Harmonically, in this section the right hand is playing triads, some with octave doubling, as well as fills from pentatonic scales. For example, in the first measure shown the E♭ major triad (with the top note G doubled an octave lower) lands on beat 1 and on the second 16th of beat 2. Later in this measure, the two-note intervals C–F, D–F, and F–B♭ can be derived from the B♭ pentatonic scale. This is in turn built from the root of the B♭ major chord, here inverted over the 3rd (D) in the bass. In the second measure shown, Elton is adding the note F on top of the second inversion C minor triad during beats 3–4. This is technically an added 4th (or added 11th) on the chord, and creates a denser, more sophisticated texture.

In the third and fourth measures shown, the F major triad (again inverted over the 3rd in the bass) begins with the top note of F in the right hand, which then moves to G (the added 9th) and then finally to A in the fourth measure. This is supported toward the end of the measure with octave-doubled F major triads. This top-note movement, together with the more intense rhythmic subdivisions, helps build the energy.

Chorus

The Chorus section builds further with strong octave roots in the left hand and octave-doubled triads in the right hand. Let's take a closer look at the second half of the Chorus, beginning on the C major chord:

Rocket Man
Example 2

For most of this section, the right-hand triads land on beats 1 and 2 and anticipate beats 3 and 4 by a 16th note. When the right hand lands on beat 2, it is preceded by another voicing a 16th note earlier (i.e., a 16th-note pickup into the downbeat). This is mostly supported in the left hand with root notes and octaves on downbeats (beats 1, 2, 3 and 4) with some eighth- and 16th-note pickups. These rhythms combine to create a lot of energy and forward motion in this chorus section.

Harmonically, the right hand makes use of triads with some octave doubling, resolutions, and added 9ths. For example, in the first measure shown, the D and F anticipating beat 3 resolve down to the C and E within the C major triad (a combined 4th-to-3rd and 9th-to-root resolution). In the second measure shown, the 9th (F) is added to the Eb major triad during beats 3–4, and in the third measure the 9th (C) is resolving to the 3rd (D) within the Bb major chord. These are all signature Elton John harmonic techniques.

In the fourth measure shown, in the right hand the 9th (F) is added as a top note on the Eb major voicing during beats 3 and 4. During beat 3 this is combined with an Ab as the bottom note, which then resolves to G (a 4th-to-3rd resolution on the chord) on the anticipation of beat 4. This temporarily creates an Eb suspended chord with an added 9th during beat 3, an interesting voicing that resolves to the following Eb major chord.

In the full song transcription, you can see that we return to another verse section after the chorus. Let's spotlight the section starting on the ninth measure of this Verse, where Elton builds a lot of energy behind the vocal line:

Rocket Man
Example 3

In the first measure shown, the right hand is playing a mix of triads and four-part shapes over the Gm7 chord. The full Gm7 four-part chord is played on beat 1 and during beat 4, and G minor and Bb major triads are played during beats 2 and 3, built from the root and 3rd of the overall Gm7 chord, respectively. Elton builds energy here by playing inversions of these triads in an ascending and descending manner, covering a two-octave range during this measure.

The feel at this point reverts to an eighth-note rhythmic subdivision, with a strong anticipation of beat 3 in both hands. Note the use of the left-hand root-7th interval, which helps to define the Gm7 chord. This a staple jazz piano left-hand device also found in more evolved pop styles. The left hand repeats the 7th of the chord (F) with the thumb later in this measure, adding forward motion to the groove.

In the second measure shown, the right hand is playing a second-inversion C7 chord on beat 1, followed by the same upper shapes (G minor and Bb major triads, and a G minor 7th four-part chord) as used in the first measure. Over the C in the bass, these collectively create a suspended dominant chord during beats 2 and 3. A similar movement between the regular (unsuspended) and suspended forms of the dominant chord occurs in the fourth measure of this section.

Overall, this verse section doesn't have a steady pulse like the first verse section we looked at; however, the eighth-note anticipation of beat 2 is played by both hands during this section (except for the second measure). This all creates an effective rhythmic contrast to the more consistent pulse felt in the following verse section.

In the full song transcription, we then observe the *D.S. al Coda* (take first ending) instruction, which takes us back to the Chorus. After taking the first ending and repeating back for the second half of the last Chorus, we then go to the Coda, a repeated two-measure phrase (or "vamp") excerpted from the Chorus.

Our next example spotlights the third and fourth measures of this final "vamp" Coda section, which moves between B♭ and E♭ major chords (I and IV within the key of B♭):

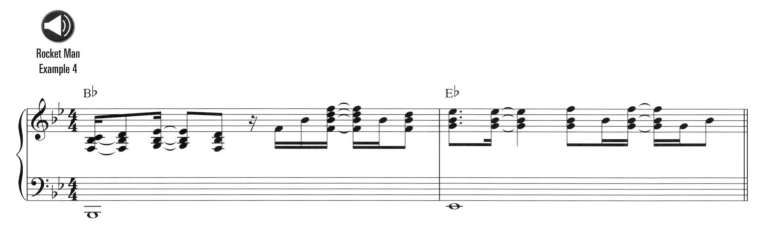

Rocket Man
Example 4

During beat 1 of the first measure shown, there is a 9th-to-3rd resolution (C to D) within the B♭ major triad played in the right hand. This is quickly followed by a IV-to-I triad movement, E♭ major to B♭ major, as a harmonic embellishment within the chord. Elton is again playing on the weak 16ths, the second and fourth 16th notes within the beat, to create his signature syncopated effect. Later in the first measure shown, the right-hand part plays arpeggios from the B♭ major chord, and then expands to an octave-doubled B♭ major triad that anticipates beat 4 by a 16th note.

In the second measure shown, the E♭ major triad in the right hand is embellished with the 9th (F) during beats 3 and 4. Again we see Elton's trademark 16th-note anticipations (landing a 16th note ahead of beats 2 and 4) in the right-hand triad and "added 9th" voicings. During beats 3 and 4, the right hand is adding partial arpeggios from the E♭ major triad, providing more subdivision and forward motion. Meanwhile, the left hand is simply playing whole-note roots, letting the right hand take the spotlight in this section.

Our final example looks at the seventh and eighth measures of the same "vamp" Coda section, which builds energy by using more intense rhythmic subdivisions:

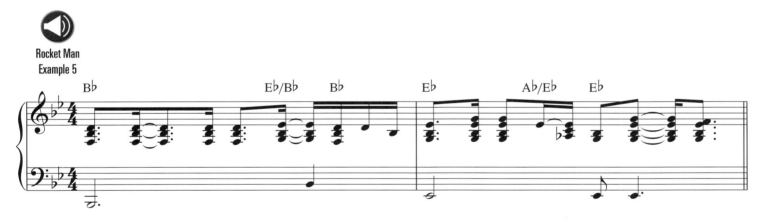

Rocket Man
Example 5

During the first measure shown, the right-hand triads are landing on beats 1 and 3, and landing a 16th note ahead of beats 2 and 4. We also have a B♭ major triad landing a 16th note before beat 3, functioning as a pickup into the triad landing on beat 3. This is a signature Elton John rhythm that imparts a lot of energy at this point.

Harmonically, the right hand in the first measure is based on a B♭ major triad, except for the brief movement to the E♭ major triad and back again (another IV–I triad movement) around beat 4. This harmonic backcycling (IV–I) idea is then repeated in the second measure shown, with the brief movement from A♭ major to E♭ major leading into beat 3, a IV–I movement on the E♭ major chord. The right hand is also strengthened with the use of octave-doubled triads and added 9ths in this measure.

Also note the strong rhythmic syncopation in the second measure shown: both hands land on the "& of 3" for the E♭ major chord, followed by the right hand playing an E♭ major chord with an added 9th (F), on the second 16th note within beat 4. These syncopations are a forceful way to punctuate the groove at this point.

Meanwhile, the left hand is playing the chord roots with simple rhythms in this example, except for landing on the "& of 3" for the two-handed syncopation described above.

Compare Examples 4 and 5 to see how Elton builds energy and intensity when vamping over a chord progression, in this case a two-measure phrase moving from a B♭ major chord to an E♭ major chord.

Rocket Man
Full Song

ROCKET MAN
(I Think It's Gonna Be a Long Long Time)
Words and Music by Elton John and Bernie Taupin

Copyright © 1972 UNIVERSAL/DICK JAMES MUSIC LTD.
Copyright Renewed
All Rights in the United States and Canada Controlled and Administered by UNIVERSAL - SONGS OF POLYGRAM INTERNATIONAL, INC.
All Rights Reserved   Used by Permission

F/A   F/G   F7   E♭add9/F

cresc.

8vb

𝄋 Chorus

B♭   E♭/B♭

And I think it's gon-na be a long, __ long time 'til touch-down brings __ me 'round a-gain to find __

Synth. Brass

Play cues on D.S. only

B♭   E♭/B♭   B♭/D

__ I'm not the man __ they think I am at home. Oh, no, __ no, no. __ I'm a

And I think it's gon-na be a long, ___ long time. ___

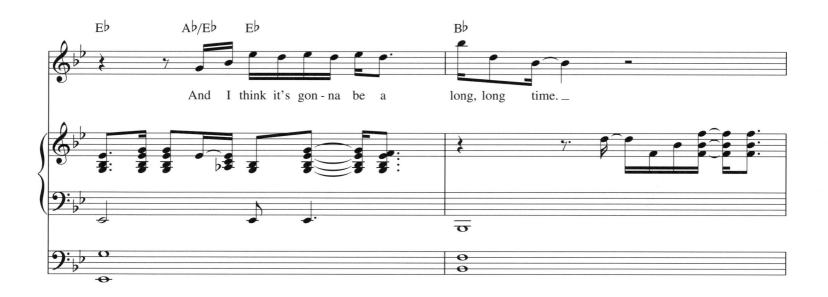

And I think it's gon-na be a long, long time. ___

And I think it's gon-na be a long, ___ long time. ___

And I think it's gon-na be a long, ___ long time. ___

Begin Fade

And I think it's gon-na be a long, ___ long time. ___

And I think it's gon-na be a long, ___ long time. ___

Crocodile Rock
(*Don't Shoot Me I'm Only the Piano Player*, 1972)

"Crocodile Rock" was a pre-release single from Elton's 1972 *Don't Shoot Me I'm Only the Piano Player* album, which (like his preceding *Honky Chateau* album) was recorded at the Chateau d'Herouville studio in France. The song was Elton's first No. 1 hit in the U.S.; it went on to be certified Platinum in 1995. It also topped the Canadian charts for four weeks in early 1972.

The song is strongly influenced by early rock songs from the 1950s and '60s, with Bernie Taupin's lyrics referencing teenage life from that period. Elton has been quoted as saying that he "wanted it to be a record about all the things I grew up with." The song is a great piece of up-tempo, light-hearted rock, and became a favorite during Elton's live concerts.

Notable covers of "Crocodile Rock" include versions recorded by the Beach Boys and the British pop singer Cliff Richard. The song was also prominently featured in the 1994 hit movie *Four Weddings and a Funeral*.

Now we'll take a look at the song section by section. For your reference, the song transcription begins on page 38.

Intro

The classic piano intro to this song has some deceptively tricky rhythms between the left- and right-hand parts. This is largely due to Elton's preference for varying rhythms when playing rock piano, rather than sticking to the repetitive patterns used by other rock pianists. Let's spotlight the eight-measure section starting on the third measure of the intro, where the song's tempo kicks in:

Crocodile Rock
Example 1

The whole song (including this Intro section) has a bright, energetic, up-tempo eighth-note feel. Little or no sustain pedal will be used, as this this would detract from the rhythmic drive and separation needed.

Note that the "8vb" written below the bass clef throughout this example, meaning that the left hand is to be transposed down an octave. This is done to avoid excessive ledger lines in the bass clef part.

Now we'll take a closer look at the interlocking rhythms used in both hands in this Intro example. We can break down these eight measures into four two-measure phrases, each of which can be rhythmically analyzed as follows:

Odd-numbered measures (i.e., first measure in each two-measure phrase)
- Left hand: playing chord roots in octaves on beats 1, 2, and 4; sometimes adding chord roots on beat 3, or on the "& of 4"
- Right hand: playing triads on the "& of 1," beats 2 and 3, and the "& of 3;" sometimes adding triads on beat 1, or on the "& of 2"

Even-numbered measures (i.e., second measure in each two-measure phrase)
- Left hand: playing chord roots in octaves on beats 2 and 4; sometimes adding chord roots on the "& of 2" (and on the "& of 3" in the last measure)
- Right hand: playing triads on beat 1 and on the "& of 2;" sometimes adding triads on the "& of 3" or on beat 4. (In the last measure shown, the rhythm is varied with more eighth-note subdivisions leading into the "& of 2," anticipating beat 3 by an eighth note)

Try playing over these two-measure phrases, then applying these comping patterns to different chords and progressions. This may be tricky at first, but is a great way to channel Elton's unique rock piano rhythms into your own arrangements!

Harmonically, the right hand is mostly playing simple triads based on the chord symbols, with the following variations in the eight-measure section shown:
- In the second measure, the right-hand thumb is repeating the bottom note of the triad (G) for some extra rhythmic subdivision; this is a common rock piano technique.
- In the fourth measure, the right hand is playing a series of harmonic 6th intervals (Gb–Eb, F–D, and E–C) that serve as a chromatic walkdown or connection between the E minor and C major chords.
- From the fifth measure onward, the right hand is playing octave-doubled triads, adding to the energy and intensity.
- In the eighth measure, the right hand briefly moves to a B minor triad on beat 2, before settling back to the D major triad on the "& of 2." This is a small harmonic embellishment within the overall D major chord in this section.

Verse

The Verse section continues the high energy level from the Intro, with right-hand triads and four-part chords, and some ornamentation and pickups. Let's spotlight the section starting on the ninth measure of the Verse, where the energy begins to pick up a little:

Crocodile Rock
Example 2

This eight-measure phrase can be broken down into a series of two-measure phrases, showing Elton's typically inventive rhythmic variations between the hands.

In the first two measures shown, the left hand is playing a blues-rock pattern using root-5th and root-6th intervals on the G major chord. However, whereas this type of pattern would normally land on all the downbeats (i.e., beats 1, 2, 3, and 4), Elton uses a much sparser rhythmic figure in the second measure shown, just landing on beat 2 and the "& of 2" (anticipating beat 3 by an eighth note). Later in the fifth and sixth measures shown, we again see left-hand root-5th and root-6th intervals played during the C major chord, this time playing a solid quarter-note rhythm throughout.

During the third and fourth measures shown (on the B minor chord), the left-hand root-5th and root-6th interval pattern mentioned above would not work; this is normally used only on major and dominant chords. So Elton instead uses a driving octave left-hand pattern here; the low B is played on beat 1 and on beat 3 or its anticipation (the "& of 2"), and the higher B is played on beats 2 and 4 (the "backbeats"), with some added eighth notes on either side of beat 4.

A similar left-hand octave pattern is used during the seventh and eighth measures on the D major chord, with a sparser rhythm in the last measure shown.

Meanwhile, the right hand uses octave-doubled triads throughout this section, as follows:
- In the first and second measures, the right hand is playing a G major triad with the 5th (D) on the top and bottom.
- In the third and fourth measures, the right hand is playing a B minor triad with the 3rd (D) on the top and bottom.
- In the fifth and sixth measures, the right hand is playing a C major triad with the root (C) on the top and bottom.
- In the seventh and eighth measures, the right hand is playing a D major triad with the root (D) on the top and bottom.

These big doubled-octave triads contribute significantly to the energy and drive of the song at this point.

Rhythmically, this right-hand part uses some interesting variations. Except in the last measure shown, the right-hand triad always lands on beat 2 (the first backbeat) in each measure. Triads also land on, or anticipate, beat 4 (landing on the "& of 3" instead of beat 4).

Also, leading into the third and fifth measures shown, the right-hand triads anticipate beat 1, landing on the "& of 4" in the preceding measure. Together with the left-hand rhythmic variations, all this combines to create a highly effective and original comping groove.

Chorus

In the full song transcription, the chorus section starts immediately after the verse we have just looked at. Now we'll spotlight the first four measures of this chorus section:

Crocodile Rock
Example 3

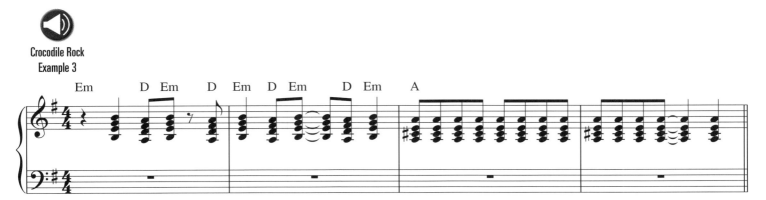

Note that this section contains only a right-hand part; rests are shown throughout the left-hand part.

Again we see the use of octave doubled triads in this chorus section:
- In the first and second measures, the right hand is alternating between an E minor triad with the 5th (B) on the top and bottom and a D major triad with the 5th (A) on the top and bottom.
- In the third and fourth measures, the right hand is playing an A major triad with the root (A) on the top and bottom.

Looking closer at the first two measures shown, we see an interesting syncopated rhythm occuring between beat 3 of the first measure and beat 4 of the second measure: this space is divided into one-and-a-half-beat increments, with the first D major triad occupying half a beat (an eighth note) and the second E minor triad occupying the remaining beat (a quarter note) within each increment. This creates an effective rhythmic figure that becomes the main hook of the chorus at this point.

During the second two measures shown, the right hand reverts to a steady eighth-note pulse when playing the octave-doubled A major triads, up until the anticipation of beat 3 in the last measure. This is then followed by a simple quarter-note rhythm, landing on beat 4, the last backbeat.

Next we'll take a look at the last four measures of this Chorus section:

Crocodile Rock
Example 4

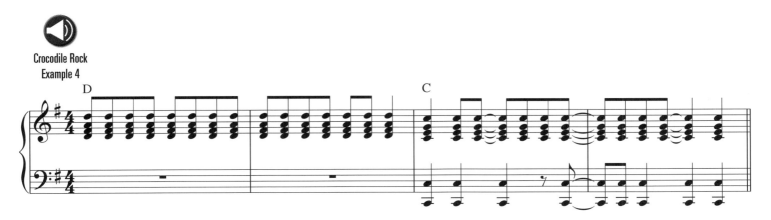

This section builds energy by using more octave-doubled triads in the right hand, as follows:
- In the first and second measures, the right hand is playing a D major triad with the root (D) on the top and bottom.
- In the third and fourth measures, the right hand is playing a C major triad with the root (C) on the top and bottom.

Rhythmically these triads are predominantly used in a steady repetitive eighth-note pattern, with some variations, such as the anticipations of beat 3 in the third and fourth measures and the anticipation of beat 1 in the fourth measure.

During the first two measures shown, the left hand is resting. Then the left hand enters in the third measure with a strong octave pattern. This is played mostly on the downbeats, again with some variations: the anticipation of beat 1 in the fourth measure, and the eighth-note pickup added before beat 2 in the fourth measure. This combines with the right-hand part in this section to produce some great syncopations between the hands.

Coda

In the full song transcription, we continue to the Interlude section, famous for its falsetto vocal melody, which uses the same chord progression as the Intro. After this, we observe the *D.S. al Coda* instruction, which takes us back to another Verse and Chorus, and then to the Coda, which repeats the falsetto vocal part. Our final example spotlights this eight-measure Coda section:

Crocodile Rock
Example 5

There are signature Elton John techniques at work in this section that build the energy level. Let's start with the octave-doubled triads in the right hand:

- In the first and second measures, the right hand is playing a G major triad with the 5th (D) on the top and bottom.
- In the third and fourth measures, the right hand is playing an E minor triad with the root (E) on the top and bottom.
- In the fifth and sixth measures, the right hand is playing a C major triad with the root (C) on the top and bottom.
- In the seventh and eighth measures, the right hand is playing a D major triad with the 5th (A) on the top and bottom.

In addition, the right hand is playing some passing triads toward the end of the fourth measure shown: D major and C major, both with their roots (D and C, respectively) on the top and bottom.

On the G major and C major chords, the left hand returns to the root-5th and root-6th interval pattern we saw earlier in the Verse section. Again we see eighth-note anticipations used over the G major chord, contrasting with the solid quarter-note rhythms used over the C major chord.

As mentioned earlier, the left-hand movement between root-5th and root-6th is not available on minor chords, so during the E minor chord Elton opts to play repeated root-5th intervals on the downbeats. This is varied with the D–A fifth interval at the end of the fourth measure shown, briefly implying a D major passing chord before the C major chord in the fifth measure.

In the last two measures of this section, the left hand is playing the root of the D major chord in octaves, which combines with the right-hand octave-doubled triads to produce a strong syncopated effect. This is achieved by dividing this two-measure section into one-and-a-half-beat increments: at the beginning of each increment, the left hand plays the root of the chord, and then an eighth-note (half a beat) later the right hand plays the octave-doubled triad. The resulting rhythmic effect is similar to what we saw in the first two measures of Example 3 earlier.

In the first six measures of this section, the right hand is primarily playing repeated eighth-note rhythms, with some variations: the anticipation of beat 3 in the second measure, and the eighth-note rests on beat 4 of the third and fifth measures, and on beat 2 of the sixth measure. These occasional right-hand rests are an effective way of varying the eighth-note rhythmic subdivision here: the rests are almost always on downbeats (beats 1, 2, 3, or 4) creating a syncopated effect with the adjacent upbeats.

CROCODILE ROCK

Words and Music by Elton John and Bernie Taupin

Crocodile Rock
Full Song

Intro
Light-hearted Rock (♩ = 148)

* *Both parts are the same synth. sound – an analog sawtooth wave sound.*

Copyright © 1972 UNIVERSAL/DICK JAMES MUSIC LTD.
Copyright Renewed
All Rights in the United States and Canada Controlled and Administered by UNIVERSAL - SONGS OF POLYGRAM INTERNATIONAL, INC.
All Rights Reserved   Used by Permission

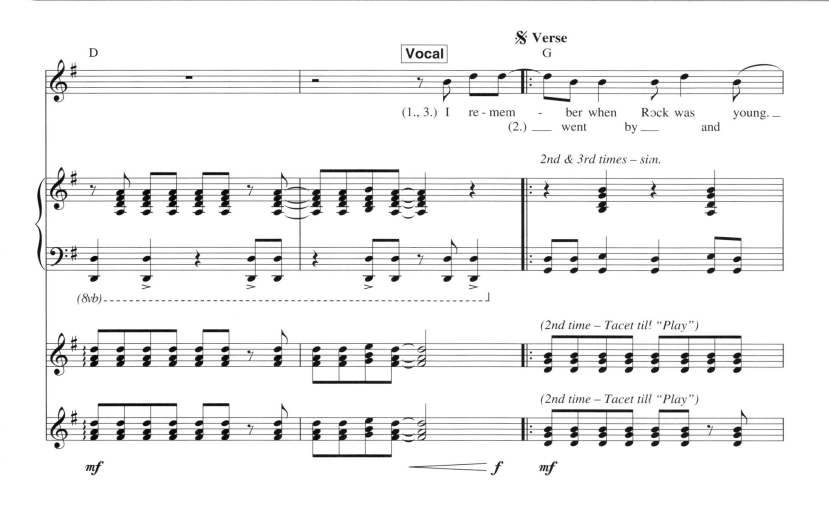

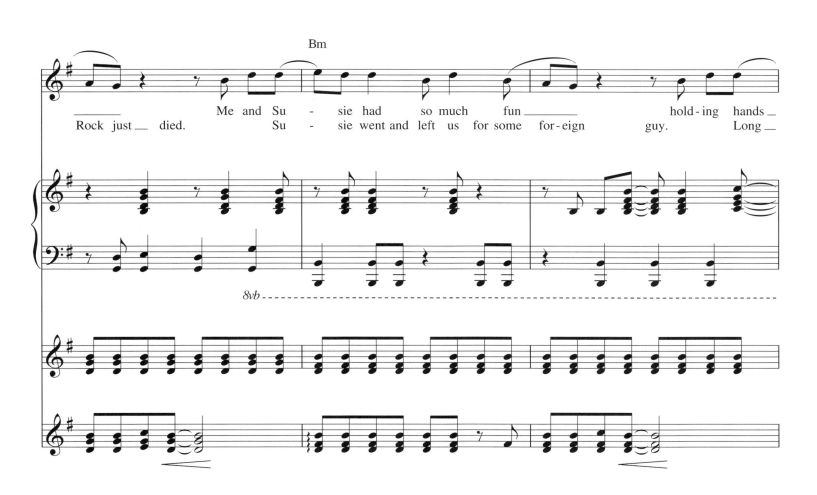

and skim-min' stones. ___ Had an old___ gold Chev - y and a
nights ___ cry - in' by the rec - ord ma - chine, ___ dream - in' of my Chev-y and my

Play Fill 1 (2nd time)

(8vb)

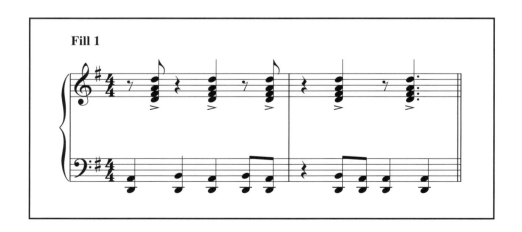

Fill 1

place of my own. _ But the big - gest kick I ev - er got _____ was do - in' a
old blue _ jeans. _____ But they'll nev - er kill the thrills we got _____ burn - in' up _

thing called the Croc - o - dile _____ Rock. _ While the oth - er kids were rock - in' 'round the
_ to the Croc - o - dile _____ Rock, learn - ing fast ____ as the weeks went past. _

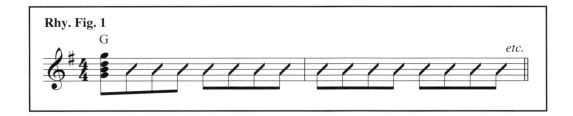

Rhy. Fig. 1

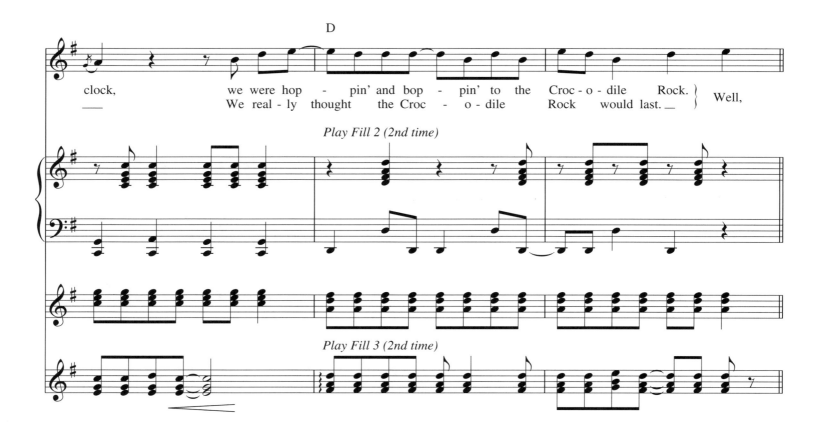

clock, we were hop - pin' and bop - pin' to the Croc - o - dile Rock.
We real - ly thought the Croc - o - dile Rock would last. ____ Well,

Play Fill 2 (2nd time)

Play Fill 3 (2nd time)

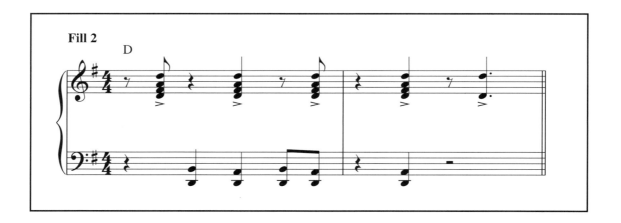

Fill 2

Fill 3

Bridge

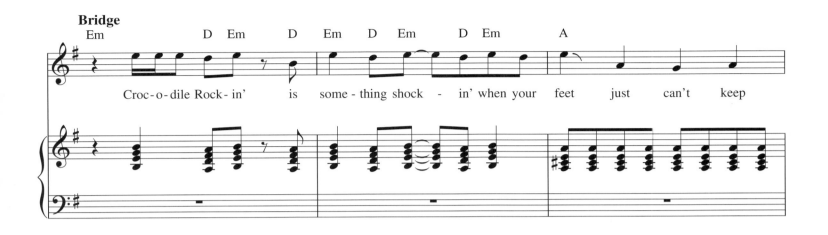

Croc-o-dile Rock- in' is some-thing shock - in' when your feet just can't keep

still. I nev - er knew me a bet - ter time __ and I guess __

____ I nev - er __ will. __ Oh, ___ lawd - y ma - ma, those

Play Fill 4 (3rd time)

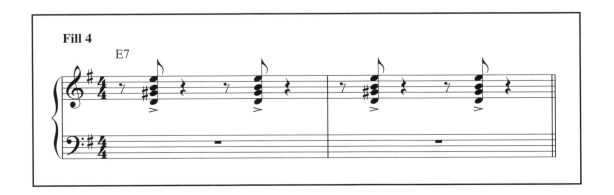

Fill 4

Fri - day nights when Su - sie wore her dress - es tight and

the Croc - o - dile Rock - in' was a - out of a - sight.

Interlude

To Coda

La, la, la, la, la,

gliss. with echo effect on downbeat

gliss.

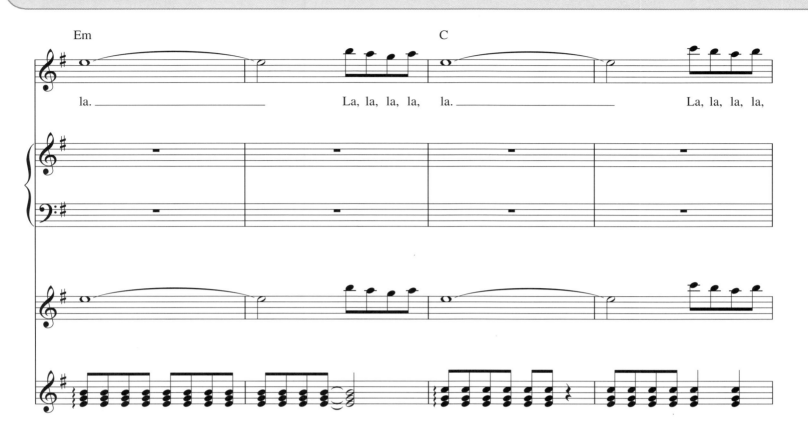

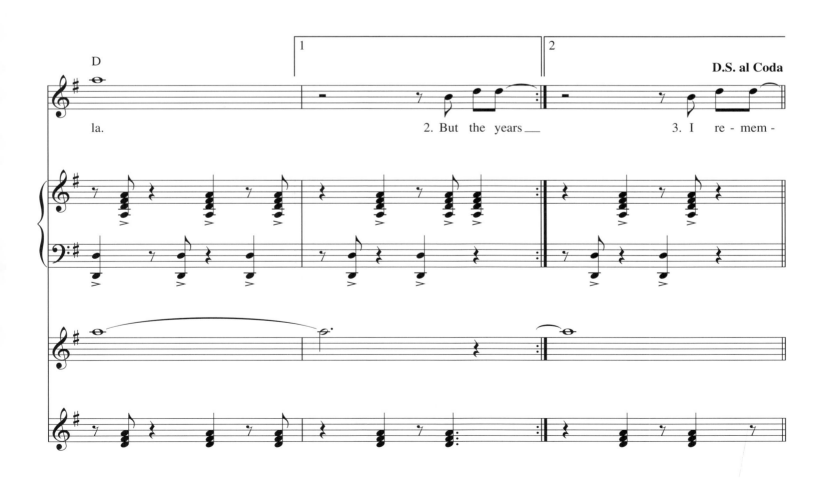

Your Song
(*Elton John*, 1970)

Elton's iconic ballad "Your Song" was originally released in the U.S. as a B-side to the single "Take Me to the Pilot." However, disc jockeys began preferring the B-side for radio airplay, which led to "Your Song" beoming a Top 10 hit on both sides of the Atlantic. Elton's piano part shows a significant Leon Russell influence, complemented by Paul Buckmaster's great string arrangement.

The song was featured on Elton's 1970 album, simply titled *Elton John*. Reportedly, Bernie Taupin wrote the lyrics over breakfast one day in October 1969, and Elton composed the complete song during a half-an-hour period later that day. When hearing the song for the first time, John Lennon was quoted as saying that it was "the first new thing that had happened since the Beatles."

While the lyric begins as a simple love song, it adds some self-deprecating touches as the narrator tries to express his feelings. Elton sings "Your Song" in most of his live concerts, and it was inducted into the Grammy Hall of Fame in 1998.

A long list of artists have covered "Your Song," including Rod Stewart, Harry Connick, Patti LaBelle, and Al Jarreau. One of the most famous performaces of the song was by Elton together with Billy Joel in October 2001, as part of a tribute show for the 9/11 attacks.

Now we'll take a look at the song section by section. For your reference, the song transcription begins on page 52.

Intro
The two-measure intro to this song is one of Elton's most classic and recognizable piano phrases:

Your Song
Example 1

With pedal

The song as a whole has a 16th-note feel, ranging from busier arpeggiated sections, as in this Intro part, to the sparser rhythms seen toward the end of the Chorus. As for most piano ballad styles, you will generally need to depress the sustain pedal for the duration of each chord.

Now we'll take a closer look at the right- and left-hand rhythms Elton is uses in each measure of this classic Intro:

*   Right hand: landing on beats 1 and 3 (the primary beats), and anticipating beats 2 and 4 (the backbeats) by a 16th note. For example, in the first measure shown, the B♭ (belonging to the E♭ major chord) is landing on the last 16th of beat 1, anticipating beat 2.
*   Left-hand pinky: playing the low root note (E♭) on beats 1 and 3.
*   Left-hand thumb: playing the root note (E♭) an octave higher than the pinky, on all the downbeats (1, 2, 3, and 4), and on the 16th-note pickups into beats 1 and 3. For example, in the first measure shown, the higher E♭ is landing on the last 16th of beat 2, picking up into the following E♭ played on beat 3.

This type of left-hand "thumb subdivision," where the left-hand thumb adds extra rhythmic subdivisions between the left-hand pinky notes, is a useful piano ballad technique. For further examples of this in action, refer to the "Stylistic DNA" section later in this book.

Next we'll take a closer look at the harmonic activity in this Intro. Note that while this section as a whole uses triadic harmony, Elton's right-hand piano part is based on only two notes of each chord at the points of chord change, beats 1 and 3 in each measure. This imparts a lighter, more delicate feel during the Intro. We can further analyze the right-hand part:

First measure
- On the E♭ chord, the right hand lands on beat 1 with the 3rd and 5th of the chord (G and B♭), before arpeggiating tones from the E♭ major chord during beats 1 and 2.
- On the A♭/E♭ chord, the right hand lands on beat 3 with the root and 3rd of the upper A♭ major triad (A♭ and C), with the A♭ being doubled one octave lower. The octave adds a little more projection here, without the density of the full triad being played. Tones from the A♭ major triad are then arpeggiated during beats 3 and 4.

Second measure
- On the B♭/E♭ chord, the right hand lands on beat 1 with the 5th and 9th of the upper B♭ major triad (F and C), with the C immediately resolving to the 3rd of the chord (D) on the next 16th note. This is a 9th-to-3rd resolution within the B♭ major triad, adding interest to the melodic line. Tones from the B♭ major triad are then arpeggiated during beats 1 and 2.
- On the A♭/E♭ chord, the right hand lands on beat 3 with the 3rd and root of the upper A♭ major triad (C and A♭). Later in the measure, when arpeggiating tones from the A♭ major triad, the 3rd of the chord (C) is doubled an octave lower.

Verse

In the full song transcription, the Verse begins right after the Intro section above, continuing the delicate 16th-note arpeggio feel. This Verse is repeated with a first and second ending, later coming back for the third and fourth ending, after the *D.S. al Coda* instruction is executed. Let's spotlight the section starting on the fifth measure of the verse, leading into the second ending. Here we see the energy level beginning to pick up a little:

Your Song
Example 2

During the first two measures shown, the right hand continues the arpeggio feel we saw earlier, in particular the anticipations of beats 2 and 4 (by a 16th note) in each measure. During beat 3 of the second measure shown, Elton is playing another 9th-to-3rd resolution, this time within a C minor triad (moving from D to E♭ within this chord). Meanwhile, the left hand is largely playing roots or other chord tones on the downbeats, with some eighth- and 16th-note pickups.

Then in the third measure shown, the right-hand energy level increases with the use of the E♭ octave-doubled triad on beat 1, and the Fm7 four-part chord (in first inversion) on beat 3. This is a significant increase in density compared to the mainly single-note patterns used in the right hand up to this point. Here the left hand also changes up, to a more solid quarter-note pattern using chord roots, and a root-5th interval on the E♭major chord on beat 1.

The fourth measure shown is a 2/4 measure with sparser rhythms: just the left-hand half-note root in octaves, together with the right-hand arpeggio. Note that Elton again makes effective use of the right-hand octave-doubled triad hand position for this sparse arpeggio – thumb on the lower E♭ and pinky on the higher E♭, within the A♭ major octave-doubled triad.

The fifth measure shown corresponds to the second ending of the Verse within the full song transcription, and builds momentum with Elton's signature mix of right-hand triads (some with octave doubling) landing on beats 1 and 3, and on the anticipations of beats 2 and 4. These are connected by arpeggio tones from the E♭ major chord in the right hand, and underpinned by a left-hand octave pattern with some eighth- and 16th-note pickups.

We also see a brief movement from A♭ major to E♭ major triads within beat 3 of this measure (a IV–I movement on the E♭ major chord), and a 9th-to-root resolution (F to E♭) at the end of the measure. These devices help build energy and lead strongly into the Chorus section that follows.

Chorus

In the full song transcription, the Chorus section starts immediately after the second repeat of the Verse that we have just looked at. Next we'll spotlight the first four measures of this Chorus section:

Your Song
Example 3

Although this section uses octave-doubled triads in the right hand and low octave roots in the left hand, there is still a fair amount of space as the rhythms are not too intensely subdivided. Note the "8vb" written below the bass clef during this example, except for the A♭ at the end of the last measure, meaning that the left hand is to be transposed down one octave.

Harmonically, the right hand is playing octave-doubled triads throughout this section, as follows:
- In the first measure on beat 1, the right hand is playing a B♭ major triad with the 5th (F) on the top and bottom.
- In the first measure on beat 3, the right hand is playing a C minor triad with the 5th (G) on the top and bottom.
- In the second measure on beat 1, the right hand is playing an F minor triad with the 3rd (A♭) on the top and bottom.
- (There is no A♭ major triad played on beat 3 of this measure. Most other pianists would have included a chord voicing here, but these variations are part of Elton's style.)
- In the third and fourth measures, the triads used are the same as for the first and second measures, this time ending with a right-hand arpeggio over the A♭ major chord.

Meanwhile, the left-hand part in this section uses octave roots on beats 1 and 3 in each measure, with some 16th-note pickups and anticipations.

Next we'll spotlight the part of the Chorus that immediately follows the previous section:

Your Song
Example 4

This section contains some interesting meter changes (4/4 to 2/4 and back again) as well as rhythmic contrasts, from dense and syncopated to sparse half- and whole-note voicings, all in the space of half-a-dozen measures.

The right-hand part in the first measure shown uses C minor triads, landing on beats 1 and 3, and anticipating beat 2 by a 16th note. As we have seen, these are typical rhythms used by Elton to build the energy level at this point in the Chorus. The left hand is supplying root notes in octaves at this point, landing on beats 1 and 3, plus the typical eighth-note pickups (on the "& of 2" and "& of 4").

Some interesting right-hand triad movements are played during beats 3 and 4 of this measure: we have a C minor triad on beat 3, a B♭ major triad on the "& of 3," and an E♭ major triad on the last 16th note of beat 3 and on the second 16th note of beat 4; the use of these weak 16ths creates an effective syncopation here. These triads all work within the Cm/B♭ chord symbol shown; however, as soon as the E♭ major triad is used, the harmonic implication shifts to an E♭ major chord inverted over its 5th (E♭/B♭).

In the second measure shown (in 2/4 time), Elton voices the Am7♭5 chord by building a C minor triad in the right hand, from the 3rd of the chord; the root is played in octaves in the left hand. This is a common chord and voicing solution in jazz styles, and is also found in more evolved pop styles – Elton occasionally makes use of m7♭5 chords in his songs. Some 3rd intervals (D–F resolving to E♭–G) are added during beat 1 to create melodic movement and interest at this point.

In the next three measures shown, Elton abruptly simplifies the rhythms down to whole-note and half-note voicings, creating an effective contrast to the preceding section. The A♭6 (A♭ major 6th) voicings simply use the root, 3rd, 5th, and 6th of the chord, with some octave doubling of the A♭. The E♭/G chord again uses an octave-doubled E♭ major triad, with the 3rd on the top and bottom. This is all supported in the left hand with root notes in octaves, creating a powerful sound overall.

In the last measure shown, Elton resumes his signature 16th-note subdivisions and anticipations, to lead into the next section. This measure is based on a B♭ major triad in the right hand, with a 4th-to-3rd resolution (E♭ to D) occuring from beats 3 to 4, briefly suspending the chord at this point.

Finally, we'll take a closer look at the instrumental section immediately following the Chorus. This is based on the Intro we saw in Example 1, with some extra bells and whistles:

Your Song
Example 5

This section adds the following right-hand variations, in comparison to the Intro section we saw earlier:

- In the first measure during beat 1, Elton plays a descending 16th-note arpeggio on the E♭ major chord, leading into the anticipation of beat 2.
- In the second measure during beat 1, the right hand plays a 9th-to-3rd resolution within the upper B♭ major triad, subtly strengthened this time with three notes (F, B♭, and C) played on the downbeat.
- In the second measure during beats 3 and 4, the right hand plays the full A♭ major triad on beat 3, followed by a filled-in octave (an octave plus another note inside) anticipating beat 4, and then a pair of parallel intervals (A♭–E♭ and C–A♭) within an octave-doubled triad hand position, all based on the A♭ major chord. This effectively builds the energy level at this point, and is a good contrast to the more delicate feel of the Intro section.

YOUR SONG

Words and Music by Elton John and Bernie Taupin

Your Song
Full Song

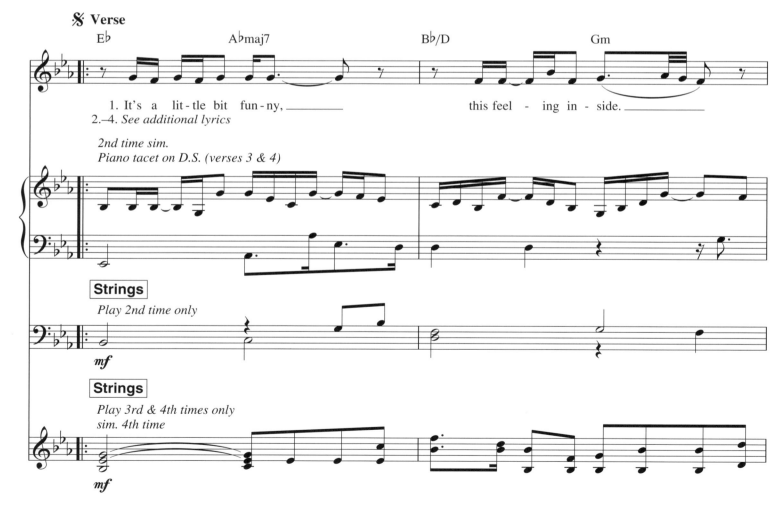

Copyright © 1969 UNIVERSAL/DICK JAMES MUSIC LTD.
Copyright Renewed
All Rights in the United States and Canada Controlled and Administered by UNIVERSAL - SONGS OF POLYGRAM INTERNATIONAL, INC.
All Rights Reserved   Used by Permission

I'd buy — a big house where — we both — could live. —

And you — can tell ev - ery - bod - y

(2nd time)

(4th time)

this __ is your song. _____ It may __ be quite ____ sim - ple, but, _____

now that it's done, _____ I hope you don't mind, ____ I hope you don't mind __

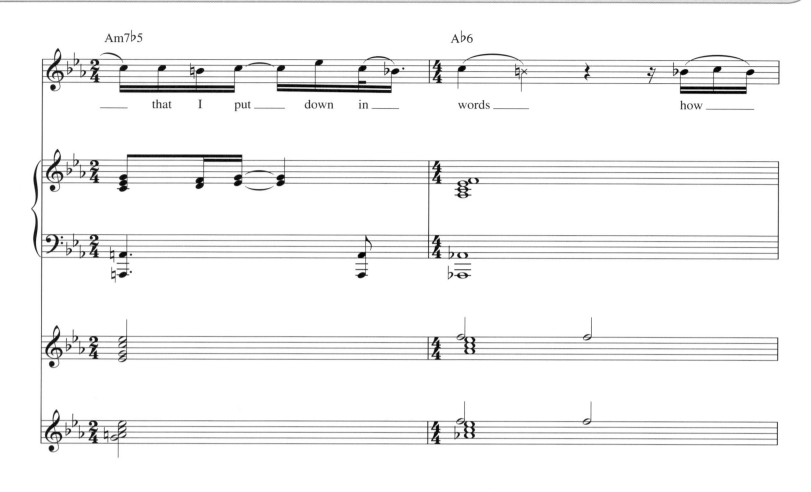

that I put ____ down in ____ words ____ how ____

won - der - ful life is ___ while you're in ___ the world. ___

(Tacet)

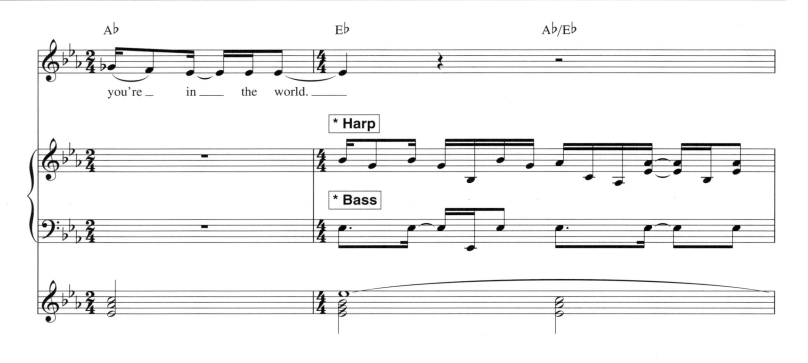

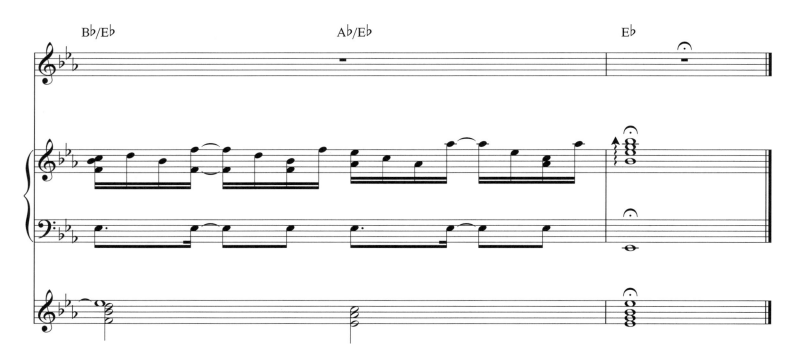

* *Piano is tacet; however, these two parts may be played on piano.*

Additional Lyrics

2. If I was a sculptor, but then again no
   Or a man who makes potions in a travelin' show...
   I know it's not much, but it's the best I can do.
   My gift is my song and this one's for you.

3. I sat on the roof and kicked off the moss.
   Well, a few of the verses, well, they've got me quite cross.
   But the sun's been quite kind while I wrote this song.
   It's for people like you that keep it turned on.

4. So excuse me forgetting, but these things I do.
   You see I've forgotten if they're green or they're blue.
   Anyway, the thing is...what I really mean...
   Yours are the sweetest eyes I've ever seen.

Sorry Seems to Be the Hardest Word
(*Blue Moves*, 1976)

Unlike most of the songs Elton has written with lyricist Bernie Taupin, the ballad "Sorry Seems to Be the Hardest Word" began with Elton playing a melody line first, inspiring Taupin's classic lyric about love and loss. The song was released as a single in 1976, becoming a Top 20 hit in both the U.S. and U.K. It was also featured on Elton's double album *Blue Moves*, released in the same year.

One of the most famous and poignant recordings of the song was a duet by Elton and Ray Charles on Ray's final album, *Genius Loves Company*, released in 1994. Ray Charles passed away just months after the recording session, and it is believed that this is the last song that he ever recorded.

Artists as diverse as Chet Atkins, Frank Sinatra, Joe Cocker, and Mary J. Blige have covered this song, and it was also prominently featured in the 1977 movie *Slap Shot*, starring Paul Newman. Elton then duetted with the boy band Blue to take the song back to the top of the charts a quarter of a century later, in 2002.

Now we'll take a look at the song section by section. For your reference, the song transcription begins on page 63.

Intro
The full song transcription shows the four-measure Intro to this song, which starts out with simple quarter-note rhythms and four-part chord voicings, leading into a delicate right-hand melody using eighth and 16th notes in the last two measures. This in turn leads into the first Verse.

Verse
Here Elton continues the quarter-note pulse used at the start of the Intro. Let's spotlight the first four measures of this Verse section:

Sorry Seems to Be
the Hardest Word
Example 1

Even though the vocal melody here has Elton's typical 16th-note subdivisions and anticipations, the piano rhythms are sparse by comparison: just quarter notes in the first and third measures where the vocal melody is active, and adding some eighth-note subdivisions in the other measures to fill in between the vocal. This overall quarter-note feel helps impart a solemn feeling to the song at this point. As seen in the previous ballad examples, you will normally depress the sustain pedal for the duration of each chord.

In the first measure shown, the right hand is playing a first-inversion G minor triad (without the root on top on beat 1), over a root-5th-root voicing in the left hand. The left hand then introduces the 7th of the chord (F) on beat 4, leading to the root-3rd voicing (C–E♭) in the second measure on the Cm7 chord.

Here the right-hand part is based on an E♭ major triad, built from the 3rd of the Cm7 chord: just two notes of this triad (B♭ and G) are played on beats 1 and 2, followed by a 9th-to-3rd resolution (F to E♭) within the first-inversion E♭ major triad on beat 3.

In the third measure shown, the right-hand F major triad on beat 1 is followed by the root only (F) on beats 2 and 3 in both hands. Then the F7 on beat 4 is voiced by building an A diminished triad from the third of the F7 chord in the right hand, over the root played in the left hand. The right hand then plays an octave-doubled B♭ major triad in the first half of the fourth measure, followed by a C minor triad which is built from the third of the Am7♭5 chord on beat 3. Again, these upper-structure triad voicings are commonly used in the more evolved pop styles.

In the full song transcription, the Verse continues in the same vein for another 12 measures, and is then followed by the Chorus section.

Chorus

Next we'll take a closer look at the first four measures of the Chorus:

Sorry Seems to Be
the Hardest Word
Example 2

Although this overall pattern looks similar to the Verse section, if we examine it more closely, we can see subtle ways in which Elton is building more intensity in the Chorus. Rhythmically, some 16th notes are introduced, in particular the second 16th of beat 2 in the right hand, in the first and third measures shown. This is a "weak 16th" and creates an effective syncopation here. Also, the right hand is using more octave-doubled triads, which (together with the left-hand octave roots) creates more momentum in the first and second measures.

Harmonically we can observe the following devices in this section:
- In the first measure during beats 1 and 2, the E♭/G is a major triad inverted over its 3rd (G) in the bass, and is played with two second-inversion E♭ major triads an octave apart in the right hand. This type of quick register change, going from low to high on the keyboard, is a favorite Elton device, used to impart energy into the arrangement.
- In the first measure during beats 3 and 4, the D/F♯ is another major triad inverted over its 3rd (F♯) in the bass, and again uses different inversions of the upper D major triad in the right hand, including an octave-doubled triad with the 5th (A) on the top and bottom on beat 4.
- In the second measure during beats 1 and 2, the B♭/F is a major triad inverted over its 5th (F) in the bass, with the right hand playing octave-doubled triads with the 3rd (D) on the top and bottom.
- In the second measure during beats 3 and 4, the C/E is another major triad inverted over its 3rd (E) in the bass, with the right hand playing an octave-doubled triad with the root (C) on the top and bottom, on beat 3. Then during beat 4, a 9th-to-3rd resolution (D to E) occurs with the C major triad, beneath G as the top note (or "drone") landing on beat 4. This phrase can be derived from the C pentatonic scale, in turn built from the root of the C major chord.
- In the third measure during beats 1 and 2, the Cm/E♭ is a minor triad inverted over its 3rd (E♭) in the bass. On beat 1 the right hand just plays the root and 5th (C and G) of the chord, creating an effective, open texture over the 3rd in the bass. Then during beat 2 the right hand moves between the 3rd and 5th (E♭–G) and root (C) of the chord.
- In the third measure on beat 3, the D7sus chord is voiced with the root and 4th (D and G) in the right hand, over the root and 5th (D and A) in the left hand. The right hand then adds an eighth-note subdivision by playing the 7th (C) on the "& of 3."
- In the third measure on beat 4, the D7 chord is voiced with the 7th and 3rd (C and F♯) in the right hand, again over the root and 5th (D and A) in the left hand. This type of "7–3" chord voicing is a jazz piano staple, which Elton uses occasionally.

In the fourth measure after the G minor chord during beats 1 and 2, more "7–3" voicings are used on the Am7♭5 and D7 chords during beats 3 and 4, with the right hand adding eighth-note subdivisions on the "& of 2" and the "& of 4."

In the full song transcription, the Chorus continues for another four measures, before leading to an Instrumental section based on the Verse:

Instrumental section

In this part of the song, Elton uses the piano to accompany an accordion and synthesizer melody. Let's spotlight the first four measures of the piano part for this Instrumental section:

Sorry Seems to Be
the Hardest Word
Example 3

This is based on the Verse section we saw in Example 1, with the following variations:
- During the first three measures shown, the right hand plays a mix of triads and two-note intervals with a steady quarter-note pulse. No eighth-note subdivisions are used until the fourth measure shown, from beat 2 onward.
- In the second measure shown, the top notes (E♭–G–F–E♭) of the right-hand intervals create an effective counter-melody over the Cm7 chord.
- From beat 3 onward in this measure, we see the left hand adding thumb subdivisions (playing the 5th of the chord as eighth notes, above the half-note root). More about this important rhythmic technique in the "Stylistic DNA" section later on.

In the full song transcription, this Instrumental section continues for another four measures, before leading to a second Chorus section:

Chorus (second)

Here we'll take a closer look at the first four measures of this second Chorus.

Sorry Seems to Be
the Hardest Word
Example 4

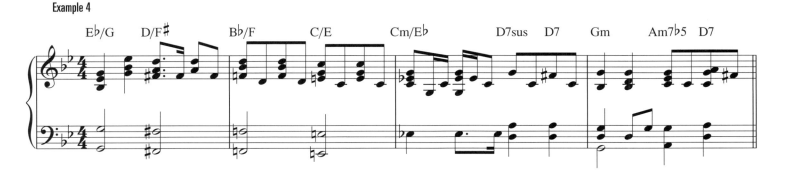

This is based on the first Chorus section we saw in Example 2, with the following variations:

- The first measure shown has some subtle rhythmic variations compared to the first measure in Example 2. After the second- and first-inversion E♭ major triads on beats 1 and 2, the right hand plays a first-inversion D major triad on beat 3, repeating the 3rd (F♯) as a 16th-note pickup into beat 4. Then during beat 4 the D major triad is split in an alternating-eighths pattern, with the 5th and root (A and D) landing on beat 4, and the 3rd (F♯) landing on the "& of 4."

- The right hand continues this alternating-eighths pattern through the second measure shown, using octave-doubled triad hand positions. For example, during beats 1 and 2 the right hand is positioned on an octave-doubled Bb major triad with the 3rd (D) on the top and bottom. The upper fingers then play the second-inversion Bb major triad on beats 1 and 2, with the thumb playing the lower D on the "& of 1" and "& of 2."

- Similar right-hand positioning is used for the octave-doubled C major triad later in this measure, during beats 3 and 4. Using alternating eighths within octave-doubled triads in this manner is a striking way to build energy in a piano ballad style.

- In the third measure shown, the right hand builds energy by playing 16th-note arpeggios on the Cm/Eb chord during beats 1 and 2. This then relaxes into an eighth-note arpeggio pattern over the D7sus and D7 chord on beats 3 and 4 of this measure.

- In the fourth measure shown, a bigger sound is created on the Am7♭5 and D7 chord on beats 3 and 4 with three-note voicings in the right hand, over root-7th and root-5th intervals in the left hand. Also, the right hand keeps the momentum going by adding eighth-note subdivisions in between (on the "& of 3" and the "& of 4").

In the full song transcription, this second Chorus leads into a Coda section that is a variation of the Verse. This is in turn followed by a four-measure instrumental final ending:

Sorry Seems to Be
the Hardest Word
Example 5

This section starts with the rhythmic feel of the Verse, using right-hand quarter-note voicings over left-hand half-note roots played in octaves. In the second measure shown, the right hand plays a 16th-note arpeggio-based figure on the Gm/D chord, which, together with the eighth-note subdivisions in the third measure, builds convincingly to the final Gm7 chord.

Harmonically, Elton is using basic four-part and triad voicings in the right hand. For example, in the first measure, the third-inversion Gm7 during beats 1 and 2, the root-position Em7♭5 during beats 3 and 4, and so on. The use of inversions in the bass allows the melodic bass line of F–E–E♭–D to be created in the first two measures shown; this is a favorite Elton John composing/arranging device, as we will see later in the "Stylistic DNA" section of the book.

SORRY SEEMS TO BE THE HARDEST WORD

Words and Music by Elton John and Bernie Taupin

Sorry Seems to Be
the Hardest Word
Full Song

Copyright © 1976 HST MGT. LTD. and ROUGE BOOZE, INC.
Copyright Renewed
All Rights for HST MGT. LTD. in the United States and Canada Controlled and Administered by
UNIVERSAL - SONGS OF POLYGRAM INTERNATIONAL, INC.
All Rights for ROUGE BOOZE, INC. in the United States and Canada Controlled and Administered by
UNIVERSAL - POLYGRAM INTERNATIONAL PUBLISHING, INC.
All Rights Reserved   Used by Permission

Accordion & vibes

Accordion & synth.

Accordion

(Electric piano ends)

Chorus

It's sad, _____ so sad. _____ It's a sad, sad sit - u - a - tion, _____

SIGNATURE PHRASES

In this section, we'll look at signature phrases or sections from another ten of Elton John's best-known songs. These sections are either taken from the Intro to the song or are a recognizable part or "hook" taken from a later part of the song – Verse, Chorus, Instrumental section, etc. These phrases are presented exactly as Elton played them on the recordings. As before, we'll explore his harmonic, rhythmic, and stylistic choices for each example.

Bennie and the Jets
(Goodbye Yellow Brick Road, 1974)

Elton recorded this song in May 1973 as part of the *Goodbye Yellow Brick Road* sessions at Strawberry Studios in France. Bernie Taupin's lyric satirizes the music industry of the 1970s, and was arguably influenced by David Bowie's work at the time. Although Elton was originally opposed to releasing the song as a single, it went on to become a No. 1 hit in the U.S.

Here we'll spotlight the classic piano Intro to this song:

Bennie and the Jets

Words and Music by Elton John and Bernie Taupin
Copyright © 1973 UNIVERSAL/DICK JAMES MUSIC LTD.
Copyright Renewed
All Rights in the United States and Canada Controlled and Administered by UNIVERSAL - SONGS OF POLYGRAM INTERNATIONAL, INC.
All Rights Reserved   Used by Permission

Note the "8vb" written below the bass clef here, indicating the left hand needs to be played an octave lower than written. These low bass notes add to the solid, heavy feel of this example. Also be sure to observe the rests, and avoid using the sustain pedal, as this would detract from the rhythmic impact needed.

Rhythmically, this Intro phrase features a strong quarter-note pulse played with both hands. This is varied with some eighth- and 16th-note subdivisions toward the end of the second and fourth measures. In the second measure, a strong syncopation is created by both hands landing on the second 16th of beat 4 (a weak 16th), particularly given the sparse nature of the surrounding rhythms. Weak 16ths are also effectively used by the left hand during beat 4 of the last measure.

Harmonically, the right hand is building minor triads from the thirds of each of the major 7th chords: in measures 1–2 the B minor triad is built from the 3rd of the Gmaj7, and in measures 3–4 the A minor triad is built from the 3rd of the Fmaj7. These triads are played in an octave-doubled style; as we have seen, this is one of Elton's favorite ways to add strength and power to the right-hand voicing. Below these triads, the left hand is playing a solid root-note alternating-octave pattern.

During beats 3–4 in the second measure, the right hand adds a melodic fill in octaves, derived from the G major scale. This is played in a higher register to contrast with the surrounding triads in the mid-range. During beat 4, an effective contrary motion is created between the hands: the right-hand octaves ascend from B to C, while the left hand descends from G to F♯. This enables Elton to connect incisively into the following Fmaj7 chord, another example of his signature melodic piano style.

Blue Eyes
(*Jump Up!*, 1982)

Elton co-wrote this song with lyricist Gary Osbourne, and recorded it during the summer of 1980. It was released as a single in 1982, reaching No. 1 on the adult contemporary charts in the U.S. The song was also included on Elton's album *Jump Up!* released in the same year. The song and its accompanying video were tributes to the actress Elizabeth Taylor.

"Blue Eyes" has a mid-tempo 12/8 feel overall, but with some interesting rhythmic variations, as we can see in the Chorus section of this classic song:

Blue Eyes

Words and Music by Elton John and Gary Osborne
Copyright © 1982 HST MGT. LTD. and BIG PIG MUSIC LTD.
All Rights for HST MGT. LTD. in the United States and Canada Controlled and Administered by UNIVERSAL - SONGS OF POLYGRAM INTERNATIONAL, INC.
All Rights for BIG PIG MUSIC LTD. in the United States and Canada Controlled and Administered by UNIVERSAL - POLYGRAM INTERNATIONAL PUBLISHING, INC.
All Rights Reserved   Used by Permission

Note that although this song is notated in 4/4 time, there are several eighth-note triplet figures used during this Chorus section. These combine to create a 12/8 feel overall. Let's look at some examples of how these eighth-note triplets are subdivided:

- In the second measure, the right hand is landing on the middle event of the eighth-note triplets during beats 2 and 4, creating a potent syncopation. This plays off the left hand landing on the first and last events of the eighth-note triplet during beat 2, outlining a swing-eighths feel at this point. The same left-hand rhythm is used during beats 2 and 4 in later measures, imparting a less repetitive, subtler swing feel to this section overall.

- In the third measure, Elton plays an interesting combination of right-hand rhythms. During beat 2, the right hand lands on the second and third events of the triplet. During beat 3, the right hand lands on the first and last events of the triplet (a conventional swing feel), with grace notes leading into the last event. During beat 4, the right hand lands on the second event of the triplet; as noted earlier, landing on the middle event here creates a useful syncopation.

- In the fourth measure, the right-hand octaves land on the middle triplet event during beats 2 and 4, again imparting a strong syncopation.

Although most of this Chorus section (and the song as a whole) makes use of eighth-note triplets, we have an important variation in the first measure: the right-hand piano line during beats 2–4 is played as straight eighths, dividing the beat exactly in half. Switching from a straight-eighths feel (dividing the beat in half) to using eighth-note triplets (dividing the beat into three parts) is not particularly common in mainstream pop styles, but Elton pulls off these rhythmic changes with panache. The piano line in the first measure also doubles the vocal melody.

Harmonically, the right hand is using a mix of upper triads and four-part shapes, with some octaves, 6th intervals, and pentatonic fills. Here are some examples of these techniques in action:

- Triads: In the first and second measures, the right hand is playing second-inversion D minor and Bb major triads, respectively.
- Upper four-part shapes: in the sixth measure, the right hand plays a Gm7b5 built from the 3rd of the Eb9 chord, and in the seventh measure the right hand plays a Gm7 built from the 5th of the Bb/C (aka C11 or C9sus) chord.
- Octaves: In the fourth and fifth measures, the right hand repeats the note C in octaves over the F/A, Fm/Ab, and G minor chords. (Arranging note: Repeating the same note through different chord changes in this way is referred to as a "pedal point.")
- 6th intervals: In the fifth measure on the G minor chord, the descending 6th intervals (D–Bb, C–A, and Bb–G) melodically lead into the following Eb chord.
- Pentatonic fills: In the third measure over the F major chord, the right-hand fills are derived from the F pentatonic scale, built from the root of the chord.

Border Song
(*Elton John*, 1970)

Elton collaborated with lyricist Bernie Taupin on this gospel-influenced ballad, though Elton himself is credited with writing the words of the last verse. The song was created and recorded in early 1970, and was released on his eponymous *Elton John* album that same year. As a single, "Border Song" was Elton's first chart success in the U.S. and Canada, although it did not fare as well in the U.K. Notable covers of the song include a version recorded by Aretha Franklin, which reached the Top 40 in the U.S.

"Border Song" blends Elton's typical 16th-note pop ballad stylings with interesting gospel influences, as we can see in the Chorus (or "hook" section):

Border Song

Words and Music by Elton John and Bernie Taupin
Copyright © 1969 UNIVERSAL/DICK JAMES MUSIC LTD.
Copyright Renewed
All Rights in the United States and Canada Controlled and Administered by UNIVERSAL - SONGS OF POLYGRAM INTERNATIONAL, INC.
All Rights Reserved   Used by Permission

This four-measure excerpt can be divided into two two-measure phrases: the first two measures that accompany the main hook of the song, and the second two measures that are essentially a repeat of the Intro section, leading into the next Verse.

The first measure uses a classic gospel-style chord progression: F major to F♯ diminished 7th to C major inverted over G. In the key of C, this is a IV–♯IVdim7–I/V movement, and is a staple of many traditional gospel songs. Note the strong quarter-note voicings used on beats 1–3 of this measure, with the right hand playing octave-doubled triads, and the left hand supporting with roots played in octaves. As we've seen before, the "8vb" notated below the bass clef means that left-hand part is to be played one octave lower than written. Again, these low octave roots show Elton's gospel piano influences.

The second measure is in 2/4 time and uses an F/G voicing that creates a G11 or G9sus (suspended dominant) chord. Here the major triad in the right hand is built from the 7th of the overall chord. This pop-friendly sound is also found in modern gospel styles. During beat 2 of this measure, the strong emphasis on the second 16th note in beat 2 (a weak 16th) creates another of Elton's trademark syncopations.

The third and fourth measures have a flowing feel, with arpeggios of the C major chord in the right hand during beat 2. However, Elton is still using 16th-note syncopations, this time landing a 16th note on either side of beat 3 (i.e., on the last 16th of beat 2, and the second 16th of beat 3), with both hands on the F major chord voicing.

Although these two measures are based on a C major chord, notice that Elton repeatedly moves to the F major chord and back again during this section. This type of I–IV–I chord movement is quite common in gospel music, and is sometimes referred to as "backcycling" in gospel circles. More about this later in the "Stylistic DNA" section.

Daniel
(*Don't Shoot Me I'm Only the Piano Player*, 1973)

"Daniel" is one of Elton John's most classic and memorable ballads. It was recorded in 1972 and appeared on the album *Don't Shoot Me I'm Only the Piano Player*, released the following year. The song reached No. 1 on the adult contemporary charts in the U.S., and was certified Gold in 1995. Bernie Taupin's poignant lyric tells the story of a veteran returning from the Vietnam War, an interesting and unusual theme for a chart-topping pop song.

In the classic piano Intro, Elton makes use of filled-in octaves in the right hand:

Words and Music by Elton John and Bernie Taupin
Copyright © 1972 UNIVERSAL/DICK JAMES MUSIC LTD.
Copyright Renewed
All Rights in the United States and Canada Controlled and Administered by UNIVERSAL - SONGS OF POLYGRAM INTERNATIONAL, INC.
All Rights Reserved   Used by Permission

Note that this example is written in "cut time;" the time signature is a C with a vertical line through it. This is equivalent to 2/2 time (i.e., two half-note beats per measure). This means that the pulse is felt on the half note, and not on the quarter note as in previous examples. Many musicians will still hear this song as having the 16th-note feel typical for Elton's ballads; notationally, though, we can choose to write it in cut time with eighth notes instead of 4/4 time with 16th notes. In this case, every two measures of cut time would be equivalent to one measure of 4/4. In other words, this eight-measure example in cut time would reduce down to four measures had it been notated in 4/4 time.

It's important to realize that these notation alternatives don't change the way the music feels or sounds; they are just different ways to represent the music. We'll have a mix of cut time and 4/4 notation examples in this book, so you should become familiar with both notation styles.

In the first four measures and the sixth measure of this example, Elton supports the Intro melody with a device I refer to as "filled-in octaves." This involves doubling the melody one octave lower, and then adding another note in between; in this case, it's a 6th interval below the top melody, or a 3rd interval above the lower octave.

For example in the second measure, the top note melody is E–D–C–B over the C major chord, which is doubled one octave lower. The "filled-in" notes G–F–E–D are then added a 6th interval below each melody note, respectively. This technique creates a bright, open texture without the power and density of octave-doubled triads.
As a variation, Elton uses right-hand triad arpeggios in the second half of this Intro section: over the G major chord (momentarily implying a suspension in the fifth measure) and over the C major chord in the seventh measure. Again we see I–IV harmonic movement used (the C to F/C chords during the last two measures). The left hand is supporting all this with minimal root-5th voicings and arpeggios in the low mid-range, contributing to the light, mellow overall feel.

Goodbye Yellow Brick Road
(*Goodbye Yellow Brick Road*, 1973)

One of Elton John's most popular and enduring ballads, "Goodbye Yellow Brick Road" is still regularly performed in his live concerts. The song was recorded in 1973 and was included on the double album *Goodbye Yellow Brick Road* released that year. A Top 10 hit in both the U.S. and U.K., the song was certified Platinum in 1995. Bernie Taupin's lyric was inspired by the classic movie *The Wizard of Oz* and by a desire to get back to the roots of life on a farm.

This example spotlights the first half of the Chorus section:

Goodbye Yellow Brick Road

Words and Music by Elton John and Bernie Taupin
Copyright © 1973 UNIVERSAL/DICK JAMES MUSIC LTD.
Copyright Renewed
All Rights in the United States and Canada Controlled and Administered by UNIVERSAL - SONGS OF POLYGRAM INTERNATIONAL, INC
All Rights Reserved   Used by Permission

Like the previous song excerpt, this one is set in cut time. Additionally, this example is to be interpreted as "swing eighths" (see the sign above the first measure). In practice, many musicians will hear this song as having a swing 16th-note feel, with each two-measure section of cut time (with swing eighths) feeling like one measure in 4/4 time (with swing 16ths). However, it's not uncommon to see this notation treatment applied to a swing-16ths type of song (i.e., double the number of measures, and using swing-eighths instead of swing-16ths), and so it will be useful for you to be acquainted with this.

Rhythmically in this example, we see that beat 3 is often anticipated by an eighth note in the right hand, which will sound like a 16th-note anticipation of beat 2 and/or 4 if you're hearing the overall 16th-note feel described previously.

Harmonically, Elton is using an interesting mix of right-hand devices in this section:
- In the first measure on the F major chord, 6th intervals are used within the octave-doubled triad: C–A and A–F. This is a simple yet useful embellishment technique.
- In the second measure on the A7 chord, the right hand is playing a second-inversion C♯ diminished triad, built from the 3rd of the chord.
- In the third measure on the B♭ major chord, the right hand is playing a 9th-to-3rd resolution within the second-inversion B♭ major triad.

Elsewhere in the right hand we see octave-doubled triads (fourth and seventh measures), basic four-part chords (fifth and sixth measures) and filled-in octaves (seventh measure). Meanwhile, the left hand keeps it simple, mostly playing roots on the half-note beats in each measure, with some rhythmic pickups.

Honky Cat
(*Honky Chateau*, 1972)

"Honky Cat" is the first cut from Elton John's *Honky Chateau* album, recorded at the Chateau d'Herouville in France and released in 1972. The single version of the song reached the *Billboard* Top 10, and is still heard on radio playlists worldwide.

The song overall has a funky, looser feel compared to some of Elton's other songs. His piano work shows the influence of New Orleans artists such as Dr. John and Allen Toussaint. The tune is noted for its energetic feel and light-hearted lyrical mood.

This example spotlights the first half of the Chorus section:

Words and Music by Elton John and Bernie Taupin
Copyright © 1972 UNIVERSAL/DICK JAMES MUSIC LTD.
Copyright Renewed
All Rights in the United States and Canada Controlled and Administered by UNIVERSAL - SONGS OF POLYGRAM INTERNATIONAL, INC.
All Rights Reserved   Used by Permission

Although this example is written in 4/4 time, many musicians will hear it as having a half-time feel, with the main pulse of the song falling on beats 1 and 3. (Please see previous comments concerning the pulse falling on the half note, for Signature Phrase #4, "Daniel.") The rhythmic comments that follow relate to how this example is notated (with eighth notes); however, if you're feeling the pulse on the half-note, then some of these rhythms will sound like 16ths. Again, this is a good exercise for familiarizing yourself with different rhythmic notation styles and preferences.

Elton's piano part here is rhythmically interesting and highly syncopated. Let's explore some of the rhythmic variations between the hands:
- In the first, fifth, and eighth measures, the right hand lands on beat 2 and the "& of 3." The left hand plays different rhythms in each case: in the first measure landing on beats 1 and 3; in the fifth measure landing on beats 1, 2, 3, and the "& of 4;" in the eighth measure landing on the "& of 1" and on beat 3.
- In the second and sixth measures, the right hand lands on the "& of 2" and on beat 4, and additionally lands on beat 1 in the sixth measure. Meanwhile, the left hand lands on beat 2 and the "& of 3" (the same rhythm used by the right hand above) in the second measure, and plays a busier octave pattern in the sixth measure.

…and so on! It's a good idea to apply these right- and left-hand rhythms to your own series of chords. That way, you'll really internalize these cool New Orleans-influenced piano comping patterns.

Harmonically, Elton is sticking with basic four-part chord voicings on the B7 and E7 chords in the right hand, cogently varied with the syncopated octaves used in the fourth measure. The left hand is generally playing chord roots as single notes or in octaves, with some eighth-note alternating octaves creating a busier feel in the second half of this section.

I Guess That's Why They Call It the Blues
(*Too Low for Zero*, 1983)

A standout song from Elton John's 1980s period, "I Guess That's Why They Call It the Blues" is a great fan favorite. With lyrics co-written by Bernie Taupin and Davey Johnstone, the song features a classic harmonica solo from Stevie Wonder. The song became a Top 5 single in both the U.S. and U.K., and was included on Elton's 1983 album *Too Low for Zero*.

The song has a relaxing, mid-tempo R&B shuffle feel, with some light blues and jazz touches, and a beautiful Intro piano melody that we'll take a look at here:

I Guess That's Why They
Call It the Blues

Words and Music by Elton John, Bernie Taupin and Davey Johnstone
Copyright © 1983 HST MGT. LTD., ROUGE BOOZE, INC. and BIG PIG MUSIC LTD.
All Rights for HST MGT. LTD. in the United States and Canada Controlled and Administered by UNIVERSAL - SONGS OF POLYGRAM INTERNATIONAL, INC.
All Rights for ROUGE BOOZE, INC. and BIG PIG MUSIC LTD. in the United States and Canada Controlled and Administered by UNIVERSAL - POLYGRAM INTERNATIONAL PUBLISHING, INC.
All Rights Reserved   Used by Permission

Note that this example is written in 12/8 time. Here the main beat or pulse falls on the dotted-quarter note. There are four of these main pulses per measure, each of which can be divided into three eighth notes. A notation alternative would have been to write in 4/4 time and to use eighth-note triplet signs to access the triplet subdivisions for each beat. (See Signature Phrase #2, "Blue Eyes.") These two songs have the same basic rhythmic feel, and Elton sometimes joins them in a medley when playing live. When working with 12/8 notation, musicians sometimes use the terms "big beat 1," "big beat 2," etc. to refer to the four main pulses in each measure.

Rhythmically, we see that the right-hand voicings are most often landing on big beats 1 and 3, with eighth-note subdivisions and syncopations in between. The left hand is pushing things along by landing on most of the big beats, with some eighth-note pickups leading into big beats 1 and 3.

Harmonically, Elton is uses a mix of right-hand devices to support the intro melody in this section:
- In the first measure on the C major chord, we start with a filled-in octave (G between the two Es). This gives a lighter, more open sound compared to an octave-doubled triad. Another filled-in octave (B between the two Ds) is used toward the end of the measure on the Em7 chord.
- In the first measure during big beats 2 and 3, the thumb is repeating the 3rd of the C major chord (E) below the melody notes D and C, and repeating the 7th of the Em7 chord (D) below the melody notes B and C. Repeating single chord tones below melody notes like this is an efficient way to define the harmony, without the density of a full triad or four-part chord.
- In the second measure on the F major chord, the right hand is playing different inversions of the F major triad below the melody, adding the 9th of the chord (G) as part of the grace note figure inside big beat 4.
- In the third and fourth measures, we see more filled-in octaves used to support the melody during the Em7 and F major chords.

In the first and third measures, a bluesy feel is created with the use of the A♯ grace note leading into the 5th of the Em7 chord (B) by half-step. The A♯ can be thought of as coming from the E blues scale, built from the root of the Em7 chord, at this point.

The left hand is playing the roots of the chords on the big beats, adding the 5th of the following chord as an eighth-note pickup at the end of each measure. In the first measure, for example, the C landing on the last eighth-note subdivision is unrelated to the Em7 chord, but is the 5th of the following F major chord in the second measure.

Little Jeannie
(*21 at 33*, 1980)

"Little Jeannie" is one of the best-known songs from Elton John's writing collaborations with lyricist Gary Osborne. It was released in mid-1980 as a single, and as part of Elton's album *21 at 33* (signifying that he had completed 21 albums by age 33), released the same year. The tune has a similar feel to his 1973 ballad hit "Daniel;" like "Daniel," it reached No. 1 on the adult contemporary charts in the U.S.

During the memorable piano Intro to this song, Elton uses various triads and intervals below the melody in the right hand:

Words and Music by Elton John and Gary Osborne
Copyright © 1980 HST MGT. LTD. and BIG PIG MUSIC LTD.
All Rights for HST MGT. LTD. in the United States and Canada Controlled and Administered by UNIVERSAL - SONGS OF POLYGRAM INTERNATIONAL, INC.
All Rights for BIG PIG MUSIC LTD. in the United States and Canada Controlled and Administered by UNIVERSAL - POLYGRAM INTERNATIONAL PUBLISHING, INC.
All Rights Reserved   Used by Permission

Note that this is another example written in cut time (two half-note beats per measure). We saw the same rhythmic notation style used for the "Daniel" example in Signature Phrase #4; please refer to the text in that section as needed. For many musicians, each two written measures of this example may feel like one measure of 4/4 with a 16th-note subdivision.

In the first eight measures of this example, we notice some anticipations of beat 3 in the melody. Then in the last four measures, we see more successive eighth-note upbeats (e.g., in measures 9 and 10), giving a more syncopated feel.

Let's take a closer look at Elton's harmonic choices in this section:
- In the first two measures, the right hand is playing a second-inversion B♭ major triad, supported in the left hand with the 5th and root (F-B♭) of the chord. In the second measure, the right hand holds the 5th and root of the triad below the eighth-note melody played above, a classic "triad below melody" technique. Similar devices are then used below the melody in measures 3–5.
- Below the melody in the sixth measure, the right hand uses diatonic 3rd intervals from the B♭ major scale. We also see this used in measures 9–10 on the E♭ major chord, this time with more rhythmic syncopation.
- In the seventh and eighth measures, the right-hand part on the Dm7 chord is based on an F major triad, built from the 3rd of the chord, with octave-doubling added in the eighth measure. Note the G-to-A movement below the top drone of C in the seventh measure; this is derived from the F pentatonic scale, again built from the 3rd of the overall Dm7 chord.
- In measures 11 and 12, the right-hand part on the E♭/F (aka F11 or F9sus) chord is based on an E♭ major triad, built from the 7th of the chord. In the last half of measure 12, this changes with the right hand re-introducing the B♭ major triad, briefly implying a B♭/F chord at this point.

During this Intro section, the left hand mostly plays a supportive role by outlining basic chord tones on the strong beats. This is varied in measures 9–10, with the left hand playing the same syncopated rhythms used in the right-hand part.

Someone Saved My Life Tonight
(*Captain Fantastic and the Brown Dirt Cowboy*, 1975)

Recorded in 1974, this Elton John classic was included on the album *Captain Fantastic and the Brown Dirt Cowboy*, released in the following year. Bernie Taupin's lyric refers to a troubled time in Elton's life in the late 1960s, when he was having serious doubts about getting married to his girlfriend at the time. The piano part on the song has a dark and foreboding quality, reflective of the serious nature of the lyrics. The song was the only single released from the album, and became a hit in the U.S., the U.K., and Canada.

Here we'll spotlight the Instrumental section following the Chorus, featuring some intense 16th-note subdivisions and left-hand bass lines:

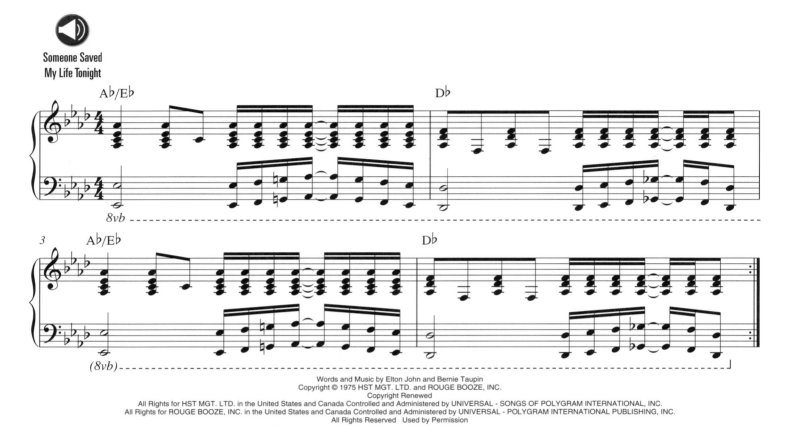

**Someone Saved
My Life Tonight**

Words and Music by Elton John and Bernie Taupin
Copyright © 1975 HST MGT. LTD. and ROUGE BOOZE, INC.
Copyright Renewed
All Rights for HST MGT. LTD. in the United States and Canada Controlled and Administered by UNIVERSAL - SONGS OF POLYGRAM INTERNATIONAL, INC.
All Rights for ROUGE BOOZE, INC. in the United States and Canada Controlled and Administered by UNIVERSAL - POLYGRAM INTERNATIONAL PUBLISHING, INC.
All Rights Reserved   Used by Permission

This four-measure section is similar to the Intro of this song. Rhythmically, it is organized around a 16th-note subdivision, like many of Elton's classic ballads. However, the intensity here results from the number of subdivisions used.

Both hands are landing on beats 1 and 3 in each measure, and anticipating beat 4 by a 16th note. Additionally, the right hand is playing an alternating-eighths comping figure (including landing on beat 2) in the first half of each measure. In the second half of each measure, both hands are landing on all the 16th-note subdivisions except on beat 4, which is anticipated.

Harmonically, there are some interesting and unusual devices. The Ab/Eb is functioning as a tonic chord, though the major triad inverted over its own 5th is not commonly used in this capacity. Also a "scale change" is occuring between the odd- and even-numbered measures: the Eb–F–G–Ab left-hand run in the first measure comes from the Ab major scale, but the Db–Eb–F–Gb run in the second measure comes from the Db major scale – or Ab Mixolydian, if we continue to reference Ab as the tonic.

In the right hand, note the strength and power resulting from the octave-doubled triads used throughout. Octave-doubled triad hand positions will be needed for the alternating-eighths comping figures on the Db major chords; for example, in the second measure the Db major triad on beat 1 should be fingered 2-3-5, allowing the thumb to play the lower note F on the upbeats. This in turn requires a rapid right-hand position change between the Ab major triad in the first measure to the Db major triad in the second measure, and so on.

Tiny Dancer
(Madman Across the Water, 1971)

"Tiny Dancer" appears on Elton John's 1971 album *Madman Across the Water* and subsequently was released as a single the following year. Although the song became a Top 20 hit in Australia and Canada, it initially failed to get much traction in the U.S. charts. Over time, however, the song became a fan favorite and radio staple. A diverse mix of artists has recorded cover versions of "Tiny Dancer," including the Red Hot Chili Peppers, Ben Folds, and Tim McGraw.

Here we'll spotlight the Chorus section of this song, featuring a number of Elton's classic 16th-note ballad comping techniques:

Tiny Dancer

Words and Music by Elton John and Bernie Taupin
Copyright © 1971 UNIVERSAL/DICK JAMES MUSIC LTD.
Copyright Renewed
All Rights in the United States and Canada Controlled and Administered by UNIVERSAL - SONGS OF POLYGRAM INTERNATIONAL, INC.
All Rights Reserved   Used by Permission

Rhythmically this excerpt uses an engaging mix of eighth-note and 16th-note subdivisions within a 16th-note ballad feel overall. The right-hand triads are either landing on downbeats (e.g., on beats 1, 2, and 3 in the first measure) or anticipating downbeats by a 16th note (e.g., anticipating beat 4 in the first measure). The right hand sometimes plays a 16th-note pickup into a downbeat (e.g., landing the last 16th of beat 2, and then also on beat 3, in the first measure).

In the second measure, the right-hand rhythms become more intense, landing on more of the weak 16ths and subdividing through beat 3, culminating in the C/E chord landing on the second 16th of beat 4; this is a strong syncopation. Likewise, the fourth measure builds with more 16th subdivisions and syncopations.

Meanwhile, the left hand is anchoring all the downbeats, with varying subdivisions used in between: eighth notes during the last half of the first and third measures, 16th-note pickups leading into beat 3 in the same measures, multiple 16th subdivisions used the second and fourth measures, and so on.

These rhythmic devices combine to create a lot of forward motion in this 16th-note ballad comping groove. Again, I suggest you work on adapting these rhythm patterns to your own progressions, to really get inside Elton's signature rhythmic approach.

Harmonically, the right hand gains strength and power from the octave-doubled triads used throughout, with occasional single notes added in between. Note the C/E chords used after the F major chords in the first and third measures, allowing the bass line to move down smoothly by half step.

In the fourth measure, the G/A (aka A11 or A9sus) chord is voiced with a major triad built from the 7th of this suspended dominant chord, a common Elton John harmonic device. The left hand is playing the root of the chords (and the bottom note of the C/E chords), reinforcing this in octaves for more power in the second and fourth measures.

INTEGRAL TECHNIQUES

In this section of the book, we'll look at some of the essential piano techniques Elton John brings to his music, including the rhythmic aspects of his unique playing style. A great deal of the drive and energy associated with Elton's playing comes from his creative use of rhythms and anticipations. Also, the big piano sound that he is noted for is due in no small part to his use of octaves in either or both hands. Here we'll delve into these areas in more detail, with supporting music examples to demonstrate each technique in action.

Left-hand octaves and octave fills

This two-measure example is in the style of Elton's comping on "Bennie and the Jets":

Techniques
Example 1

In many of Elton's songs, we see left-hand octaves used to define the root of each chord, often in the low register, showing a gospel piano influence. In the first measure of this example, the left hand plays the root of the A minor 7th chord (A) in octaves on beats 1 and 3, the primary beats in 4/4 time. Similarly, in the second measure, the left hand plays the root of the E minor 7th chord (E) again on beats 1 and 3.

The left hand is also playing the root and 5th of the chord during beats 2 and 4 in each measure, in a rhythmic conversation with the right-hand part. For example, during beat 2 the left hand lands on the second and fourth 16th notes. These weak 16ths land on either side of the right-hand triad that is sounded halfway through beat 2; this creates a funky, syncopated effect. The left hand also plays the 5th of each chord on beat 4, followed by the root on the last 16th note, which functions as a pickup into the following downbeat.

Meanwhile, the right hand is playing major triads built from the 3rds of each of the minor 7th chords; C is built from the 3rd of the Am7, and G is built from the 3rd of the Em7. The right-hand rhythmic pattern is classic pop/R&B; it lands on beat 1, the last 16th of 1, the "& of 2," the "& of 3," and on the second 16th of beat 4. This all adds up to a funky 16th-note groove. Again, you are encouraged to apply this comping pattern to other chord progressions and songs!

Next up we have a four-measure example in the style of Elton's comping on "Crocodile Rock":

Techniques
Example 2

This four-measure example breaks down into two two-measure phrases (measures 1–2 and 3–4), both rhythmically and harmonically.

Here we see an interesting mix of upbeats and downbeats in the left-hand octave figure. (To recap: The "downbeats" are beats 1, 2, 3, and 4 in 4/4 time; the "upbeats" are the eighth-notes in between, i.e., the "& of 1," "& of 2," and so on.)

In the first and third measures, after landing on beat 1, the left hand lands an eighth note ahead of beat 3, and beat 1 in the following measure. Anticipating the primary beats in this way creates a strong syncopated effect. The left hand is also landing on the backbeats (2 and 4), which function as pickups into the following anticipations.

This is balanced out in the second and fourth measures, with the left-hand octaves landing on all the remaining downbeats (beats 2, 3, and 4).

Meanwhile, the right hand creates an effective counter-rhythm to these left-hand octave figures. In the first and third measures, the right hand joins the left hand on beat 2 for a strong backbeat, preceded by a eighth-note pickup, and then lands on the "& of 3," which anticipates beat 4. Then against the steady left-hand downbeats in the second and fourth measures, the right-hand chords land on the last three upbeats ("& of 2", "& of 3", and "& of 4") in the second measure, and on the middle two upbeats ("& of 2" and "& of 3") in the fourth measure.

All this combines to create an original and arresting resultant rhythm between the two hands on this comping groove, as opposed to the more repetitive patterns often heard in pop/rock songs with an eighth-note rhythmic subdivision.

Harmonically, the right hand is simply playing major triads corresponding to the chord symbols, using octave doubling for extra weight and power. Note the repeated single eighth notes played by the right-hand thumb at the beginning of the second and fourth measures; these extra thumb subdivisions impart energy and forward motion to the groove. (More about left-hand thumb subdivisions later on, in the "Stylistic DNA" section.)

Finally for this left-hand octave technique, we have a three-measure example in the style of Elton's intro figure and comping on "Don't Let the Sun Go Down on Me":

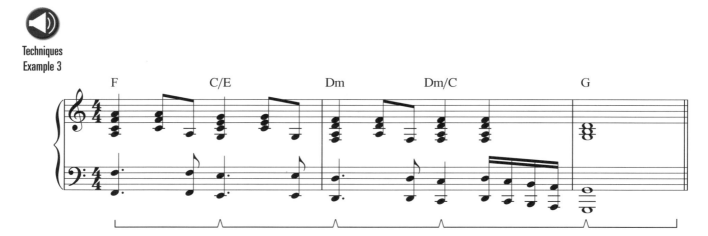

Techniques
Example 3

Here the left-hand octave figure is using a common eighth-note ballad rhythm in the first measure and the first half of the second measure, landing on beats 1 and 3 (the primary beats) preceded by eighth-note pickups (on the "& of 2" and the "& of 4"). Then on beat 4 of the second measure, the left hand switches to playing a consecutive 16th-note figure in octaves, connecting stepwise from D down to G, the root of the final G major chord. This persuasively builds intensity leading into the G major chord, and is a common Elton John left-hand device. (He plays a similar figure in "Someone Saved My Life Tonight," as we saw earlier in Signature Phrase #9.)

Over these changes, meanwhile, the right hand is playing a classic alternating eighth-note pattern within octave-doubled triads. For example, in the first measure the F major triad (octave-doubled with A on the top and bottom) lands on beat 1, and is then split during beat 2, with the upper fingers playing the F triad (C–F–A) on the downbeat, and the thumb playing the lower A on the upbeat. A similar pattern occurs within the C/E chord during beats 3–4, and so on. On beat 4 of the second measure, the right hand simply plays a quarter-note octave-doubled triad; any further subdivision might be too much, given the busier left-hand figure at this point.

When playing this example, maintain the octave interval around the triads in the right hand, and use the sustain pedal as indicated. It's a matter of preference as to how much sustain pedal to use across the left-hand 16th-note figure in the second measure; blending these notes together will sound muddy, yet the pedal can add to the size and impact of the sound. Let your ears be the judge!

Right-hand octaves and octave fills

Elton John's use of octave figures and fills in the right hand is one of the signature ways in which he builds energy and motion into his playing. First we'll look at a four-measure example in the style of his comping on "Goodbye Yellow Brick Road":

Techniques
Example 4

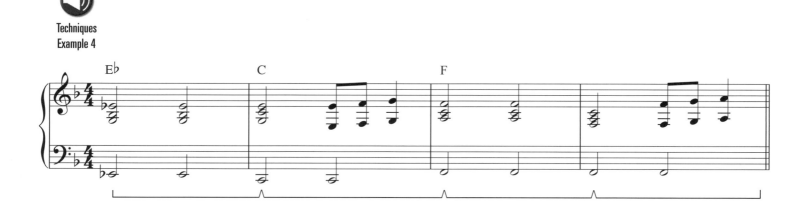

Here we see a fairly simple use of octave fills in the right hand, during beats 3–4 of the second and fourth measures. The comping pattern is built on two half-note voicings per measure, and the octave fills provide the only quarter- and eighth-note subdivision. As such, these fills really stand out due to their busier rhythm.

Harmonically, this type of octave fill is often used to connect between chord tones in the right hand. In the second measure, the right hand plays the third of the C major chord (E) on beat 3, passes through the connecting tone F on the "& of 3," then lands on the fifth of the chord (G) on beat 4. Similarly, in the fourth measure, the right hand plays the root of the F major chord (F) on beat 3, passes through the connecting tone G on the "& of 3," then lands on the third of the chord (A) on beat 4. The connecting tones are normally taken from the major scale of the key signature, F major in this case.

As with most piano ballad styles, the sustain pedal is used for the duration of each chord. You can decide whether to blend the notes of the octave fills together using the pedal: this would not be unusual, even though some dissonance can arise from combining adjacent notes in this way.

Next we have a four-measure example inspired by Elton's syncopated right-hand octave fills on "Honky Cat":

Techniques
Example 5

This four-measure example shows the bluesy side of Elton's playing, with interesting cross-rhythms between the hands, and use of blues scales in octaves in the right hand.

Although this example is written in 4/4 time, it will most likely be heard as having a half-time feel, with the main pulses falling on beats 1 and 3 in each measure. This is consistent with how Signature Phrase #6 (excerpted from "Honky Cat") is notated earlier in this book.

Rhythmically, the left hand is landing on all the main pulses, playing an octave-root note pattern for both the G major and C major chords. During the second and fourth measures, the left hand is landing halfway through beats 3 and 4. These syncopations will sound like 16th-note upbeats if we're feeling the main pulse on the half note.

The right-hand rhythms will have a similarly funky effect, in particular landing halfway through beats 2, 3, and 4 in the second measure, and halfway through beats 1, 2, and 3 in the last measure. Also during the third and fourth measures, more alternating rhythms are used between the hands, with the right-hand octaves landing in the spaces between the left-hand pattern. All this contributes to the New Orleans-influenced funky groove created here.

During the first measure and the first half of the second measure, the right-hand octave run G–A–Bb–B–D–E–G comes from the E blues scale; E is the relative minor of the key of G, which this piece is in. (This sequence of notes is also referred to as a "G major blues scale" in some textbooks.)

Then from the second half of the second measure through to the third measure, the right-hand octave run D–C#–C–Bb–G comes from the G blues scale, built from the tonic of the key (G). This type of blues scale mixing, using blues scales from both the tonic and the relative minor of the key, is a common blues device.

In the fourth measure, the right hand Eb–E movement is a b3rd-to-3rd resolution within the C major chord, another signature blues sound. (The right-hand notes in this measure could also be sourced from the A blues scale.)

Lastly for this right-hand octave technique, we have a two-measure example in the style of Elton's signature fills on "Rocket Man":

**Techniques
Example 6**

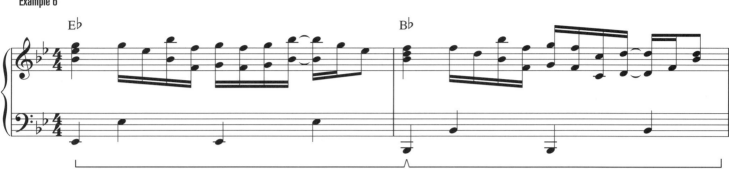

This example has the 16th-note rhythmic subdivision that characterizes Elton's pop ballad style. The right-hand figure is anticipating beat 4 of each measure by a 16th note, and otherwise is subdividing throughout beats 2, 3, and most of beat 4 in each measure. Apart from the right-hand anticipation of beat 4, both hands are landing on all the downbeats (i.e., 1, 2, 3 and 4).

Harmonically, the right hand is playing simple triads on beat 1 of each measure, followed by an arpeggio and octave figure starting on beat 2 of each measure.

In the first measure, during the first half of beat 2, the right hand is playing a partial arpeggio of the Eb major triad, the notes G and Eb. Then starting halfway through beat 2, the right hand plays the octave figure Bb–F–G–F–G–Bb as continuous 16th notes. This run comes from the Eb pentatonic scale, built from the root of the chord. Then during beat 4, another partial arpeggio of the Eb major triad is used, this time the notes G–Eb.

Similarly in the second measure, during the first half of beat 2 the right hand is playing a partial arpeggio of the Bb major triad, F and D. Then starting halfway through beat 2, the right hand plays the octave figure Bb–F–G–F–C–D as continuous 16th notes. This run comes from the Bb pentatonic scale, again built from the root of the chord. During beat 4, a second-inversion Bb major triad is split, with the bottom note (F) landing on the second 16th of beat 4 and the top two notes (Bb and D) landing immediately afterward on the "& of 4."

This combination of triads, arpeggios, and pentatonic scales in octaves creates a simple yet compelling ballad groove typical of Elton's style.

Left-hand pickups into downbeats

Playing left-hand pickup notes into downbeats is one of the most powerful ways that pop and rock pianists can impart forward motion into their comping. Elton John is a master of this important rhythmic technique.

A "pickup" here is defined as a rhythmic event that occurs immediately before a downbeat (either beat 1, 2, 3, or 4 of a 4/4 measure), which is then followed by another rhythmic event on that downbeat. Pickups are normally played either an eighth note or 16th note ahead of a downbeat, depending on the rhythmic style of the song.

Most Elton John songs, particularly his ballads, have a 16th-note feel, so pickups in these songs would normally be a 16th note ahead of the downbeat. The most common beats to be preceded by a pickup in this way, are beats 1 and 3, the primary beats in 4/4 time. However, Elton typically uses pickups into any or all the beats in a measure.

To see these principles at work, we'll first look at a four-measure example in the style of Elton's comping on the verse of "Border Song":

Techniques
Example 7

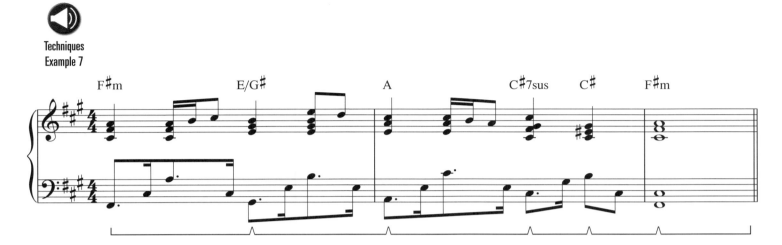

Here we see consistent left-hand rhythmic pickups; all the downbeats, except beat 1 in the first measure, are preceded by 16th-note pickups. Try playing this example without these 16th notes; you can hear a significant loss of energy and motion when the pickups are removed. As a variation, we have an eighth-note pickup into beat 1 of the third measure, which has a smoother, less intense rhythmic effect.

In general, this type of left-hand pickup will either repeat the previous left-hand note, normally the root of the chord, or it will add harmonic definition by playing another note within the current chord. In this example, the pickups notes are part of the "open triad arpeggio" patterns in the left hand, a common harmonic device in piano ballad styles.

For example during beats 1 and 2 in the first measure, the left hand pattern is F#–C#–A–C#, a root-5th-3rd-5th pattern on the F# minor chord. The term "open triad" is used because the 3rd of the chord (A) has been transposed up one octave, resulting in the triad now having a range larger than one octave overall.

During beats 3 and 4 in the first measure, the left-hand pattern is G#–E–B–E, a 3rd-root-5th-root pattern on the E/G# chord, a major triad inverted over its 3rd in the bass.

This left-hand part is combined with a simple right-hand part: mostly basic triads played on each downbeat, with top-note movement during beats 2 and/or 4 in each measure. This a straightforward, useful piano ballad template that you can apply to many songs!

Next up we have a two-measure example in the style of Elton's rhythmically forceful comping on "Somebody Saved My Life Tonight":

Techniques
Example 8

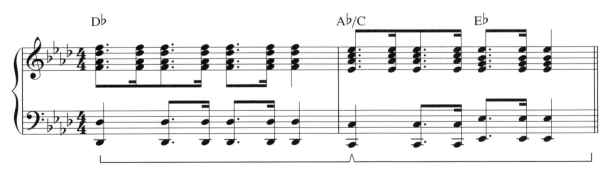

This example contrasts effectively with the previous one, in that it has much more intensity and power. This is in part due to the left-hand pickups being played in octaves, leading into downbeats that are also played in octaves. Also, the root of each chord is more heavily emphasized, as the pickup notes are simply repeating the root (rather than playing other parts of the chord as in the previous example).

Rhythmically, the left hand (in addition to landing on all the downbeats) is playing pickups into beats 3 and 4 in each measure. This combines with the right-hand part that also lands on all the downbeats, and plays pickups into beats 2, 3, and 4 in each measure. With the exception of the pickup into beat 2 in the right hand, the same rhythms are played between the hands, contributing to the forceful effect.

The octave-doubled triads used in the right hand are also an important contribution to the energy of this example. In the first measure, we have a D♭ major triad, with the 3rd of the chord (F) on the top and bottom. In the second measure, during beats 1 and 2 we have an A♭ major triad with the 5th of the chord (E♭) on the top and bottom; during beats 3 and 4 we have an E♭ major triad with the root of the chord (E♭) on the top and bottom.

Finally for this left-hand pickup technique, we have a four-measure example in the style of Elton's comping on "Bennie and the Jets":

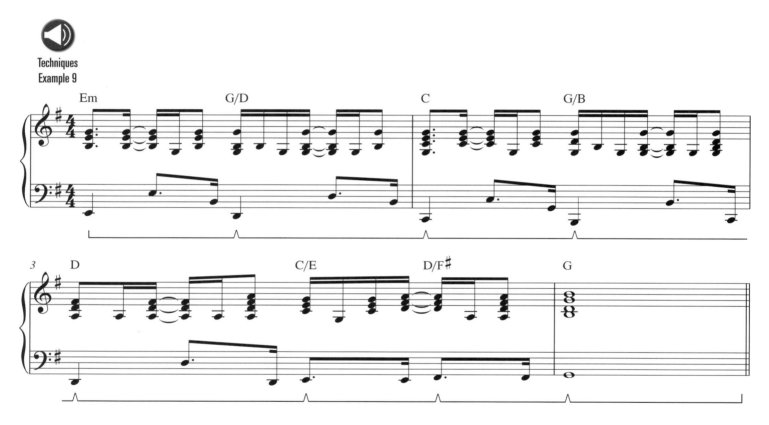

Techniques
Example 9

In this excerpt, the left hand plays the roots of the chords on the downbeats: in the lower octave on beats 1 and 3, and in the higher octave on beats 2 and 4, except for beat 4 in the third measure. In between, the left-hand pickups lead into beats 1 and 3, with an extra pickup leading into beat 4 in the third measure. This time the pickups are not repeated root notes of the chords; instead, they are either another chord tone of the current chord, or a melodic connection into the root of the following chord.

In the first measure, for example, the left hand plays B (the 5th of the Em chord) on the last 16th note of beat 2, leading into the D on beat 3 needed for the G/D chord. In the second measure, the left hand plays C on the last 16th note of beat 4, leading into the D on the following beat 1. Here, the C is not part of the G/B in measure 2, but connects stepwise into the D in the next measure.

Meanwhile, the right hand is anticipating beats 2 and 4 by a 16th note in the first three measures, which (together with the left-hand part landing on these downbeats) helps create Elton's signature R&B-influenced ballad sound. Elsewhere, the right-hand part is landing on the second and third 16ths within beats 2 and 4, and subdividing all the 16ths within beat 3.

Harmonically, the right-hand part is based on triads, with some octave doubling. When playing this example, an octave-doubled triad hand position is recommended for the right-hand part. For example, on the Em chord in the first measure, play the first triad with the upper fingers of the right hand (2-3-5), with the thumb positioned on the G below middle C, which will be needed during beat 2. On the following G/D chord, the right-hand thumb and pinky will again be on the two Gs on either side of middle C, and so on.

Right-hand anticipations

A key ingredient of rock and R&B piano styles is the use of rhythmic anticipations in the right hand. Elton John uses this particular technique quite productively. To recap: An anticipation occurs when a rhythmic event lands ahead of the downbeat (beats 1, 2, 3, or 4) and is then either followed by a rest or is sustained through the following downbeat. This has the psychological effect of shifting the beat earlier, by either an eighth note or a 16th note, generating rhythmic momentum in the piano part.

When this right-hand technique is used, the left hand will still most often land on the following downbeat, meaning that the right hand will land earlier than the left hand at this point. This requires good rhythmic independence between the hands to execute successfully.

First we'll see this technique at work in a 16th-note ballad style, reminiscent of Elton's playing on the the Intro to "Your Song":

Techniques
Example 10

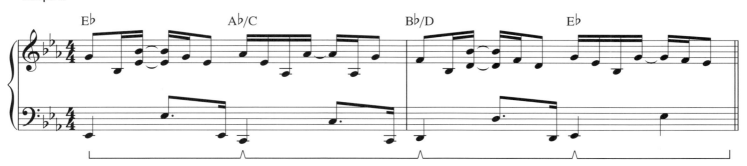

Most of Elton's ballads have a 16th-note rhythmic subdivision. One of his favorite ballad comping techniques is to anticipate beats 2 and/or 4 in the right hand by a 16th note. Here, the right hand anticipates beats 2 and 4 in each measure, using either a single note or a partial triad (two notes) according to the chord symbols.

In general, the more notes that are played on the right-hand anticipation, the greater the emphasis or syncopated effect that is created. This example is rather delicate in nature, as there are only one or two notes played on the anticipations. In later examples in this section, though, we see a more forceful effect created by using three or four notes at once – normally a triad or octave-doubled triad, respectively.

For most of this right-hand part, I recommend an octave-doubled triad hand position. For example, on the first E♭ major chord, the thumb would be on the lower B♭ and the pinky on the higher B♭, with the second and third fingers on the E♭ and G in between, respectively. This approach will be the most efficient as we move from chord to chord. We can take a closer look at the right-hand arpeggios and anticipations in this example, as follows:

- First measure on the E♭ chord: the 3rd and 5th of the chord (G and B♭) land on beat 1 and the "& of 1," followed by the root and 5th together (E♭ and B♭) anticipating beat 2 by a 16th note. In beat 2, the 3rd and root of the chord are played (G and E♭).
- First measure on the A♭/C chord: the root-5th arpeggio (A♭–E♭–A♭–A♭) uses all the 16th subdivisions in beat 3, with the last A♭ anticipating beat 4 by a 16th note.
- Second measure on the B♭/D chord: the 5th and root of the chord (F and B♭) land on beat 1 and the "& of 1," followed by the 3rd and root together (D and B♭) anticipating beat 2 by a 16th note. In beat 2, the 5th and 3rd of the chord are played (F and D).
- Second measure on the E♭ chord: the triad arpeggio (G–E♭–B♭–G) uses all the 16th subdivisions in beat 3, with the last G anticipating beat 4 by a 16th note.

Meanwhile, the left hand is playing the root of each chord in alternating octaves, on all the downbeats, with additional 16th-note pickups into beat 3 of the first measure, and into beats 1 and 3 of the second measure. (See Techniques Examples 7–9.)

Next we have a more energetic four-measure example inspired by Elton's comping style on "Rocket Man":

Techniques
Example 11

This four-measure example is a representative slice of Elton's 16th-note piano ballad style, with multiple right-hand anticipations using triads and four-part chords, as well as arpeggios, chordal resolutions, and a left-hand mix of roots and root-5th intervals on downbeats, with some 16th-note pickups.

Looking at the second measure in this excerpt, we see a right-hand anticipation technique similar to our first example in this section, anticipating beats 2 and 4 by a 16th note and with the left hand landing on these downbeats. However, in the first measure we see a rhythmic variation: the note C (the root of the C minor triad) is played on beat 2, followed by the full C minor triad landing on the second 16th of beat 2.

This is a weak 16th and essentially functions as an anticipation of the "& of 2." In other words, this creates a strong rhythmic "kick" (syncopation) at this point. Landing on the second 16th of the beat in this way is a favorite Elton John technique, as we have seen in earlier examples, and is a noticeable contrast to the more typical anticipations of beats 2 and 4.

Harmonically, let's take a closer look at the right-hand part:
- First measure on the Cm chord: a second-inversion C minor triad is played on beat 1 and during beat 2 as described above, separated by a partial triad arpeggio, the notes G and C.
- First measure on the B♭/D chord: The right-hand part is based on an octave-doubled B♭ major triad, with F on the top and the bottom. A 9th-to-3rd resolution (C to D) occurs within this chord, at the start of beat 2. (Again, note that all the 16th-note subdivisions within beat 3 are used, leading into the anticipation of beat 4.)
- Second measure on the E♭ chord: First- and second-inversion E♭ major triads are played on beat 1 and the last 16th of beat 1 (anticipating beat 2), respectively. Playing different successive right-hand triad inversions in this way is another of Elton's favorite right-hand techniques. Later, during beat 2, a 9th-to-root resolution (F to E♭) is occurring on the E♭ major chord.
- Second measure on the Fm7 chord: A first-inversion Fm7 four-part chord is played on beat 3, the last 16th of beat 3 (anticipating beat 4), and halfway through beat 4. On the second 16th of beat 4, the right hand plays the lowest note of the chord (A♭) as a thumb pickup into the last chord voicing on the "& of 4."

The left hand is playing solid root-5th voicings on beat 1 of each measure, on the Cm and E♭ chords, and playing the root of each chord on all the other primary beats (2, 3, and 4). Again note the sparse but efficacious use of 16th-note pickups in the left hand, leading into beat 3 of each measure.

Finally for this right-hand anticipation technique, we'll look at a two-measure example inspired by Elton's forceful comping on the Chorus of "Tiny Dancer":

**Techniques
Example 12**

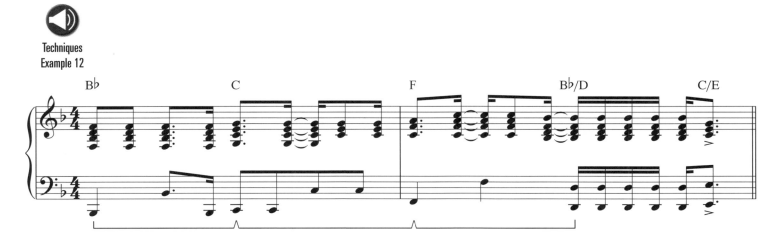

This example showcases several ways in which Elton John imparts high energy to his 16th-note ballads when needed:
- Repeated use of octave-doubled triads in the right hand
- Use of 16th-note pickups and anticipations in both hands
- Multiple 16th-note subdivisions in both hands during beat 3 of the second measure
- And so on

Regarding the right-hand anticipation technique we are focusing on here: We see this at work in the first measure, anticipating beat 4 by a 16th note, and in the second measure, anticipating beats 2 and 3 by a 16th note. Also, both hands land on the second 16th of beat 4 in the second measure, creating a strong syncopation. (This weak 16th is technically an anticipation of the "& of 4" in this measure.)

Also, there is some striking rhythmic interplay between the hands during the C major chord (beats 3 and 4) in the first measure. After landing on beat 3, the right hand then lands on a series of weak 16ths: the last 16th of beat 3 (anticipating beat 4), and then the second and fourth 16ths of beat 4. The left hand adds an eighth-note pulse at this point (landing on beat 3, the "& of 3," beat 4, and the "& of 4") which alternates and interlocks quite effectually with the right-hand part. The right hand uses a similar rhythmic figure during the first half of the second measure on the F major chord, this time with the left hand playing a simple root-note pattern in octaves.

Harmonically, the right hand is playing triads (mostly octave-doubled) according to the chord symbols in this example, which, together with the left-hand octaves and busy rhythms, combines to create this high-energy 16th-note comping groove.

Two-handed syncopations

In this book we've already seen several examples of anticipations (playing ahead of the beat), particularly in the right hand. (See the preceding Integral Technique.) Now we'll move on to more advanced uses of anticipations in both hands, creating what could be termed "two-handed syncopations." Elton John's rhythmic comping style often features simultaneous rhythmic variations in both hands, rather than always sticking to a repetitive comping pattern, and this naturally leads him into combining these multiple syncopations between the hands.

These patterns can be deceptively tricky to play, and you may need to practice these parts hands separately before combining them together. Good hand independence is essential to be able to play these examples correctly.

First we'll see this technique at work in a funky 16th-note rock style, reminiscent of Elton's comping on "Bennie and the Jets":

Techniques
Example 13

This example has multiple eighth- and 16th-note anticipations in the right hand, with some weak or syncopated 16th notes being added by the left hand in the rhythmic spaces between the right-hand voicings. This is a common rhythmic keyboard technique across a range of R&B/pop/funk styles.

In each measure of this example, the right-hand triads land on beat 1, the last 16th of beat 1, the "& of 2," the "& of 3," and the second 16th of beat 4. Apart from the triad landing on beat 1, these all function as either eighth- or 16th-note anticipations. We can take a closer look at these:

- Triad on the last 16th of beat 1: This is a weak 16th and is a 16th-note anticipation of beat 2, creating a highly syncopated effect.
- Triads on the "& of 2" and the "& of 3": These are eighth-note anticipations of beats 3 and 4, respectively. These are lighter and less intense syncopations compared to the anticipation of beat 2 above.
- Triad on the second 16th of beat 1: This is another weak 16th and is technically a 16th-note anticipation of the "& of 4," again creating a pronounced syncopation.

Against this, the left hand is landing on all the downbeats, with some weak 16ths added in between, including some 16th-note pickups, in a rhythmic alternation with the right-hand part.

Harmonically, the right hand is alternating between G and D major triads (built from the 3rd and 7th of the E minor 7th chord) in the first measure, and between A minor and G major triads (built from the 3rd and 9th of the F major 7th chord) in the second measure.

The left hand is playing the root of each chord in an octave pattern, with the 5th of each chord added as a pickup into beat 3 of each measure.

Next we have a highly syncopated four-measure example inspired by Elton's comping style on "Honky Cat":

Techniques
Example 14

Although this example is written in 4/4 time, it will most likely be heard as having a half-time feel, with the main pulses falling on beats 1 and 3 in each measure. This is consistent with how Signature Phrase #6, excerpted from "Honky Cat," is notated earlier in this book.

Rhythmically, the left hand is landing on all the main pulses (beats 1 and 3), except for beat 3 in the fourth measure. However, between each pulse there is considerable variation in the rhythmic subdivisions. Also, each time a note lands halfway through the beat and is then followed by a rest, this will feel like a 16th-note upbeat or weak 16th, given the overall half-time feel of this example. See earlier comments following Techniques Example 5.

Now we'll take a closer look at these left-hand rhythmic variations in each measure. The following comments relate to the 4/4 notation used for this example:
- First measure: The left hand lands on beats 1, 2, and 3, then on the "& of 3" (anticipating beat 4) and on the "& of 4" (picking up into the following beat 1).
- Second measure: The left hand lands on beat 1 and the "& of 1" (anticipating beat 2), and then on all of the subdivisions from beat 3 onward (i.e., beat 3, the "& of 3," beat 4, and the "& of 4").
- Third measure: The left hand lands on beat 1, and then on all the subdivisions from beat 2 onward (i.e., beat 2, the "& of 2," beat 3, the "& of 3," beat 4, and the "& of 4").
- Fourth measure: The left hand lands on beat 1, and on the "& of 1" (anticipating beat 2), the "& of 2" (anticipating beat 3), and the "& of 3" (anticipating beat 4).

By itself, this left-hand part is not at all repetitive, and the varying anticipations in each measure contribute to the funky effect. On top of this, we also have different right-hand rhythms in each measure, as follows:
- First measure: The right hand lands on beats 2 and 3.
- Second measure: The right hand lands on beat 1, on the "& of 2" (anticipating beat 3), and on beat 4.
- Third measure: The right hand lands on the "& of 1" (anticipating beat 2), on beat 3, and on the "& of 4" (anticipating beat 1 in the following measure).
- Fourth measure: The right hand lands on beat 2 and on the "& of 3" (anticipating beat 4).

When combining this continually varying right-hand rhythmic part with the above left-hand rhythmic variations, a unique and funky series of "two-handed syncopations" is created.

Harmonically, the right hand is playing some four-part upper structure voicings on the dominant chords:
- On the C13 chord in the first and second measures, the right hand is playing a B♭maj7♭5 upper shape, built from the 7th of the overall chord.
- On the G9 chord in the third and fourth measures, the right hand is playing a Bm7♭5 upper shape, built from the 3rd of the overall chord.

These are common upper-structure voicings for dominant chords in jazz and blues styles.

The left hand is either playing the root of each chord, or alternating between root-5th and root-6th intervals on the chord. This is another device borrowed from blues styles, and works particularly well on dominant chords.

Finally, for this "two-handed syncopations" technique, we'll look at another four-measure example, this time inspired by Elton's energetic comping on "Crocodile Rock":

Techniques
Example 15

This up-tempo straight-eighths pattern again has rhythmic variations and syncopations in both hands. We can break this example down into two two-measure phrases, which have some rhythmic similarities and differences:

Left hand
- In the first and third measures, the left hand is landing on beats 1, 2, and 4, and also on the "& of 2" (anticipating beat 3) and the "& of 4" (anticipating beat 1 in the following measure).
- In the second and fourth measures, the left hand is landing on beats 2, 3, and 4.

Right hand
- In the first and third measures, the right-hand voicings are landing on beat 2, and also on the "& of 1" (picking up into beat 2) and the "& of 3" (anticipating beat 4). Additionally, in the third measure, the right hand is landing on beat 3.
- In the second and fourth measures, the right-hand voicings are landing on the "& of 2" (anticipating beat 3) and the "& of 3" (anticipating beat 4). Additionally, in the second measure the right hand is landing on the "& of 4" (anticipating beat 1 in the following measure), and in the fourth measure the right hand is landing on beat 1.

The right hand is also playing a single note with the thumb in the second and fourth measures, on the "& of 1" and on beat 2, further adding to the subdivision and forward motion of this comping pattern.

Again, these varying syncopations in the combined left- and right-hand parts, impart a lot of energy and originality to this groove. They are signature Elton John rhythmic techniques.

Harmonically, the right hand is mostly playing octave-doubled triads, with some interior chordal movements of I–IV–I on each chord (e.g., the movement from C to F and back to C again during the first two measures). There's more to come on these right-hand "backcycling" triad movements, in Stylistic DNA (pages 95–97).

STYLISTIC DNA

In this section of the book, we'll dig deeper into some of Elton John's harmonic and melodic stylings on the piano. These are some of the common musical threads that run through his playing and writing, and help identify his piano style to our ears. Here we'll take a closer look at Elton's use of right-hand triads and intervals, and some of the ways he creates harmonic embellishments and variations, among other things. As for the earlier sections in this book, we'll have supporting music examples to demonstrate each DNA point in action.

Right-hand "backcycled" triads

"Backcycling" is a term used to describe I–IV–I (or IV–I) triad movements within a chord progression. This is often done as a harmonic embellishment technique, and is a staple device in gospel and rock piano styles. Our first backcycling example is in the style of Elton's comping on "Border Song":

DNA
Example 1

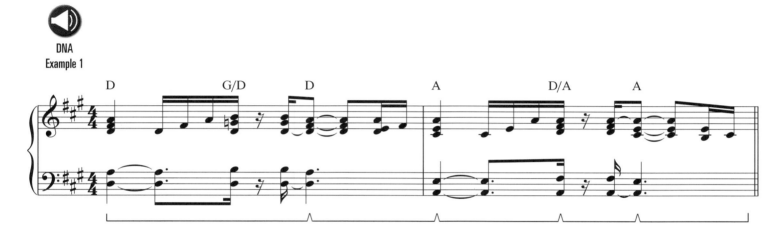

Harmonically, the first measure is based on a D major chord, and the second measure is based on an A major chord. However, in the middle of the first measure, we move from D to G/D and back to D, a I–IV–I movement with respect to the D major chord. Similarly, in the middle of the second measure, we move from A to D/A and back to A, a I–IV–I movement with respect to the A major chord. This is a classic backcycle in action, and is a signature part of Elton's sound.

Note that the IV chord in the middle of each backcycle is placed over the root of the original chord. For example, in the first measure, the G chord is placed over D in the bass, which is the root of the D major chord. This is the most typical way in which backcycling is applied, although it's possible for the IV chord simply to have its own root in the bass, moving from D to G and back again to D.

The right hand is also playing a chordal arpeggio leading into each backcycle, as well as a 9th-to-3rd resolution during beat 4 of each measure. For example, in the first measure, the 9th of the D major chord (E) resolves to the 3rd (F♯) during beat 4. Meanwhile, the left hand is supporting the right-hand part with root-5th and root-6th intervals during each measure.

Rhythmically, we see some of Elton's typical syncopations in this example. In each measure, both hands "lock up" on the last 16th of beat 2 (anticipating beat 3), and also on the second 16th of beat 3. The use of these successive weak 16ths creates a noticeably syncopated effect here.

Next up we have a four-measure example in the style of Elton's comping on the verse of "I Guess That's Why They Call It the Blues":

DNA
Example 2

This example is written in 12/8 time. Here, the main pulse falls on the dotted-quarter note. There are four of these main pulses ("big beats") per measure, each of which can be divided into three eighth notes. This notation is consistent with how Signature Phrase #7 (excerpted from "I Guess That's Why They Call It the Blues") is notated earlier in this book.

If we look at the right-hand part in the first measure, we can see that on big beats 1 and 3 the right hand is playing a G major triad, and on big beats 2 and 4 the right hand is playing a C major triad. The C major triads here are a backcycling embellishment on the overall G major chord that is in force during this measure.

This movement continues into the first half of the second measure and is followed by the G major triad anticipating big beat 4, and then by the F and C major triads that signal the backcycling to come on the C major chord. Then in the third and fourth measures, we have a similar backcycling movement, this time between the C and F major triads, as we saw in the first two measures.

Note that the chord symbols are simply G for the first two measures, and C for the last two measures (rather than showing G, C/G, G, C/G, etc. in the first measure). Sometimes you will see these more "general" chord symbols that do not reflect the backcycling chord movements, and sometimes you will see chord symbols assigned to the backcycling movements (as in DNA Example 1 on page 95).

Finally, for this backcycling technique, we have a four-measure example in the style of Elton's comping on "Saturday Night's Alright for Fighting":

DNA
Example 3

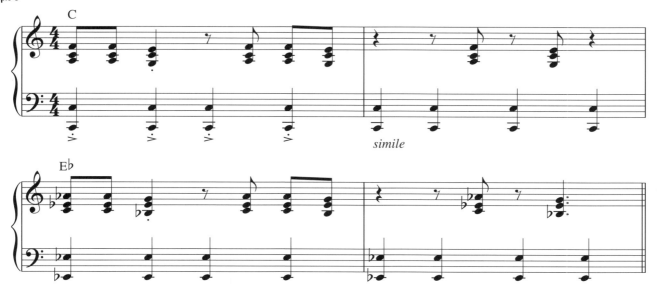

This example is typical of Elton's high-energy pop/rock comping. Here we see backcycled triads used over the C major chord in the first two measures, and over the E♭ major chord in the last two measures. More detail on this, as follows:

- In the first measure, the right hand plays an F major triad (in first inversion) on beat 1 and the "& of 1," before resolving to the C major triad (in second inversion) on beat 2. This is a IV–I backcycle movement on the C major chord. The same right-hand rhythmic figure is then repeated, starting on the "& of 3" and finishing on the "& of 4" in this measure. This is a good example of rhythmic displacement – taking the same rhythmic figure and repeating it at different starting points in the overall phrase.
- A similar IV–I backcycled triad movement, A♭ major triad moving to E♭ major, then occurs over the E♭ major chord in the third and fourth measures.
- Meanwhile, the left hand is playing a solid root-note pattern in octaves on all the downbeats (1, 2, 3, and 4). This drives the groove along and is a strong support to the backcycled triads and syncopations in the right hand.

Right-hand octave-doubled triads

As we have seen in earlier examples, an octave-doubled triad is one in which the top note has been doubled an octave lower, resulting in a four-note shape whose overall span is one octave. This is often done to add weight and power in the right hand, and is a critical element in Elton John's piano toolbox. Our first octave-doubled triad example is in the style of Elton's comping on "Someone Saved My Life Tonight":

DNA
Example 4

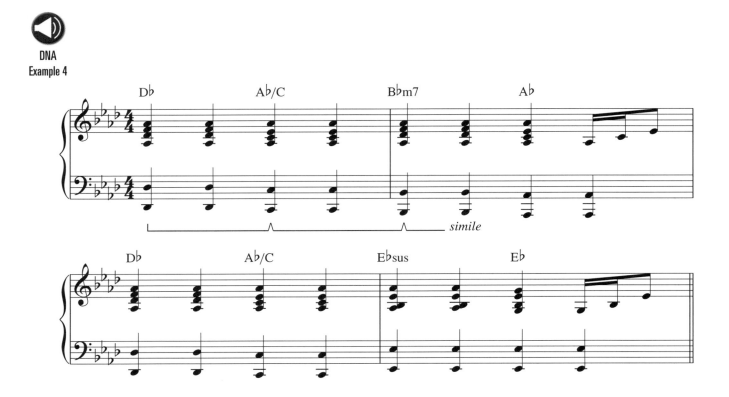

Here, the right hand is playing octave-doubled triads on all the downbeats in the first and third measures, on beats 1–3 of the second measure, and on beat 3 of the fourth measure. During the first two beats of the fourth measure, the right hand is playing a suspended E♭ major triad (B♭–E♭–A♭), with the top A♭ doubled an octave lower. These powerful right-hand voicings are accompanied by strong left-hand octaves playing the root notes of each chord (except during the last two beats of the third measure, where the left hand is playing the third of the A♭ major chord).

In the first half of the second measure, the D♭ major triad in the right hand is built from the third of the overall B♭m7 chord. Rhythmically, both hands are playing a steady quarter-note rhythm throughout, except for the right-hand arpeggio during the last beat of the second and fourth measures. This overall example shows a simple yet powerful use of right-hand octave-doubled triads at work.

Next up we have a two-measure example in the style of Elton's playing on the Interlude section of "Tiny Dancer":

DNA
Example 5

This 16th-note ballad example showcases a number of Elton John's piano devices, including the right-hand octave-doubled triads on beat 1 of each measure. These are followed by 16th-note octave fills connecting between chord tones of the E♭ major and C minor chords.

For example, the E♭ major octave-doubled triad (with E♭ on the top and bottom) on beat 1 of the first measure is followed by the octave fill of E♭–F–G that connects between the root (E♭) and third (G) of the chord. Similarly, the C minor octave-doubled triad on beat 1 of the second measure is again followed by the octave fill of E♭–F–G, this time connecting between the third (E♭) and fifth (G) of the chord.

During beat 3 of each measure in the right hand, we see a 9th-to-3rd resolution (C to D) within a B♭ major triad, using an octave-doubled triad hand position (with F on the top and bottom). The B♭ major triad is used for two different harmonic purposes: during the first measure the B♭ major chord is placed over its 3rd (D) in the bass, while in the second measure the B♭ major triad is built from the 3rd of the overall G minor 7th chord.

Meanwhile, the left hand is playing a series of two-note interval voicings: root up to the 5th on the E♭, Cm, and Gm7 chords, and 3rd up to the root on the B♭/D chord.

Rhythmically, the right hand is landing on all the downbeats, except for the 16th-note anticipation of beat 4 in each measure. The left hand is landing on all the downbeats, with 16th-note pickups into beat 2 of each measure. These anticipations and pickups are true-to-type for Elton's ballad style.

Finally, for this octave-doubled triad technique, we have a four-measure example in the style of Elton's comping on "I Guess That's Why They Call It the Blues":

DNA
Example 6

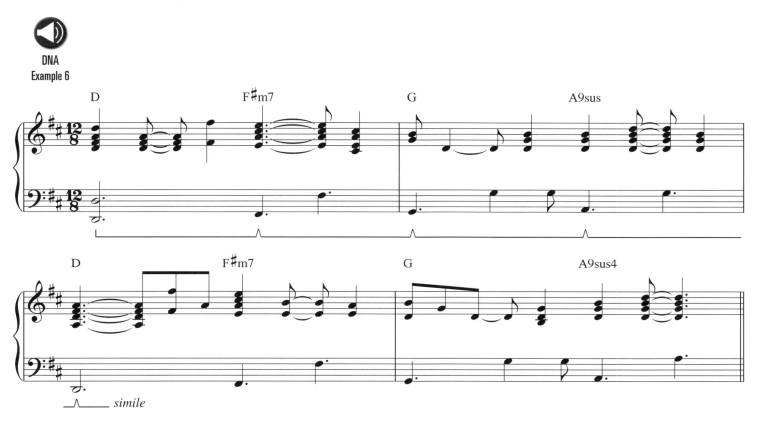

As with previous examples based on this classic Elton John song, the notation is written 12/8 time, with the main beat or pulse falling on the dotted-quarter note. There are four of these pulses (sometimes referred to as "big beats") in each measure.

This example is strengthened with various right-hand octave-doubled triads.

First and third measures
- On big beat 1, the right hand plays an octave-doubled D major triad, with D on the top and bottom in the first measure, and with A on the top and bottom in the third measure.
- On big beat 3, the right hand plays an octave-doubled A major triad, built from the 3rd of the F♯ minor 7th chord.

Second and fourth measures
- On the anticipation of big beat 4, the right hand plays an octave-doubled G major triad, built from the 7th of the A suspended dominant 9th chord.

Toward the end of the first measure, the octave-doubled A major triad is repeated in a different inversion, this time with C♯ on the top and bottom. Elsewhere, we see non-octave-doubled triads in the right hand, as well as a 4th-to-3rd resolution (B to A) on the F♯m7 chord in the third measure, and an arpeggio of the G major triad at the start of the fourth measure. The left hand is supporting all this with a simple root-note octave pattern throughout.

Rhythmically, we see an interesting use of the triplet subdivisions available within each big beat in 12/8 time. The right hand is often landing on the last triplet subdivision within big beats 1 and/or 3, anticipating the following downbeat. By contrast, the right hand is often landing on the middle triplet subdivision within big beats 2 and 4. Meanwhile, the left hand is landing on all the big beats, with eighth-note pickups into big beat 3 during the second and fourth measures. All this combines to create great forward motion in this 12/8 comping style.

Right-hand 3rd and 6th intervals

The use of 3rd and 6th intervals in the right hand is an important technique for the pop piano player, particularly in ballad styles. These intervals are used either as a melody support device or as a way to embellish comping patterns. Thirds and 6ths have a harmonically warm, consonant quality and are useful across a range of pop music styles. These intervals are most often played in stepwise ascending or descending patterns, and are normally diatonic to (i.e., belong to) the key of the song.

Although these 3rd and 6th intervals are by no means unique to Elton John's playing, he makes impressive use of this technique, as we will see in this section. Our first right-hand interval example is in the style of Elton's classic Intro on "Little Jeannie":

DNA
Example 7

Here, we are using a series of diatonic 3rd intervals in the right hand to support the melodic figure in the second and fourth measures. For example, in the second measure the first three right-hand top notes are C♯, D, and E, and below this top line the notes A, B, and C♯ are added, respectively. This creates a series of 3rd intervals (A–C♯, B–D, C♯–E, and so on) that are diatonic to the key of A major.

Similarly, in the fourth measure, the first three right-hand top notes are B, C♯, and D; below this top line the notes G♯, A, B are added, again creating a series of diatonic 3rd intervals. The use of the consecutive 3rd intervals in this example has a tight, compact sound, compared to the broader, larger sound of the 6th intervals in the next example.

Rhythmically, we see the right hand is anticipating beat 3 in the second and fourth measures, landing an eighth note ahead of the left hand in each case.

The left hand is playing the chord roots in an octave pattern in the first and third measures (anticipating beat 3), and simple two-note intervals on beats 1 and 3 in the other measures. From bottom to top, these intervals are either 3rd-root (on the A/C♯ chord), root-5th (on the D and A chords), or the root played in octaves (on the continuation of the E chord in the fourth measure).

Next, we have a four-measure example reminiscent of Elton's comping fills between the first and second verse on "Daniel":

DNA
Example 8

Note that this example is written in cut time, with two half-note beats per measure. This is consistent with how Signature Phrase #4, excerpted from "Daniel," is notated earlier in this book.

In the second measure, the right hand uses a descending series of 6th intervals. Beginning halfway through beat 1, the right-hand top notes are C, B, A and G, and below these the notes E, D, C and B are added, creating a series of diatonic 6th intervals. Similarly, after the F major triad arpeggio in the third measure, the descending melodic line of F, E, D, C and B again has 6th intervals added below. These successive right-hand 6th intervals have a broad, warm, consonant effect.

Rhythmically, the right-hand use of consecutive eighth-note anticipations is typical for Elton. For example, in the third measure the right hand lands on the "& of 2" and the "& of 3," and in the third and fourth measures the right hand lands on all of the "&s" (upbeats) between the "& of 2" in each of these measures. These all impart a gentle yet telling syncopation in this ballad-oriented style.

The left hand is playing a mix of root notes, root-5th intervals, and root-5th-root arpeggios, again with Elton's trademark rhythmic variations. For example, the root-5th voicings an eighth note on either side of beat 1 in the second measure are quite syncopated for this mellower type of groove; elsewhere, the left hand lands on beats 1 and/or 3 of each measure, with some anticipations of beats 2 and 3.

Finally, for this right-hand interval technique, we have a three-measure example in the style of Elton's comping on "Don't Let the Sun Go Down on Me":

DNA
Example 9

This example adds more energy in the right hand with the use of octave doubling, together with 3rd and 6th intervals. For example, during beat 4 of the first measure, the melodic line (E to F) is not only supported with 3rd intervals below (C to D), but the top notes E and F are also doubled one octave below.

Similarly, in the last half of beat 2 of the second measure, the melodic line (E to D) is not only supported with 6th intervals below (G to F), but the top notes E and D are also doubled one octave below. This technique is also referred to as "filled-in octaves," i.e., an octave with another note in between.

This has a transparent yet powerful effect, and is one way in which Elton imparts a gospel flavor to his pop piano stylings.

Elsewhere we see some familiar Elton John harmonic and rhythmic techniques:
- The right-hand backcycled triads (I–IV–I) in the first measure; see Stylistic DNA Point #1
- The left-hand 16th-note pickups into downbeats (i.e. beats 2 and 4) in the first measure; see Techniques Examples 7–9 (pages 87–88)
- The right-hand E diminished triad on beat 4 of the second measure; this implies a C7 dominant chord inverted over its 3rd (E), leading into the following F major chord; this is a common blues and gospel device

Left-hand "thumb subdivisions"

Here, left-hand "thumb subdivisions" refers to a technique in which the left hand pinky is holding a note down for one or more beats, while the left-hand thumb adds more rhythmic subdivisions on top. This is a subtle yet persuasive way of imparting forward motion to the rhythmic groove.

Elton John is not the only player to employ this technique, of course. For example, Paul McCartney makes good use of it on the "Let It Be" piano part. However, Elton uses it particularly well in both eighth-note and 16th-note rhythmic styles.

Our first left-hand thumb subdivisions example is in the style of Elton's comping on the verse of "Sorry Seems to Be the Hardest Word":

DNA
Example 10

This example has an eighth-note rhythmic feel, and here the left-hand thumb subdivisions are adding eighth-note upbeats that function as pickups into the downbeats played by the right hand. For example, in the last half of the first measure, the left hand pinky is holding the root (C) of the Cm7 chord for two beats. The left-hand thumb plays the fifth (G) of the chord above, not only on beat 3 (together with the pinky) but also on the "& of 3" and the "& of 4."

These extra subdivisions function as pickups into the following downbeats, adding subtle extra momentum to the comping pattern. A similar technique is used on the last half of the second measure (on the Fm7 chord), and on the first half of the last measure (on the E♭sus chord).

We see a variation of this idea being used in the third measure; the left-hand root-7th of the B♭7sus chord (B♭–A♭) lands on beat 2, with the lower B♭ being held down for the remainder of the measure. The left-hand thumb then restrikes the 7th (A♭) on the "& of 3," followed by the 5th (F) on the "& of 4."

Meanwhile, in the first three measures the right-hand thumb repeats one chord tone in each measure, which supports a moving line played by the upper fingers. For example, in the first measure, the thumb plays the 7th of the Cm7 chord (B♭) on all the downbeats, below the upper line of E♭, G, F, etc.

Next we have a three-measure example, written in the style of Elton's comping on the verse of "Rocket Man":

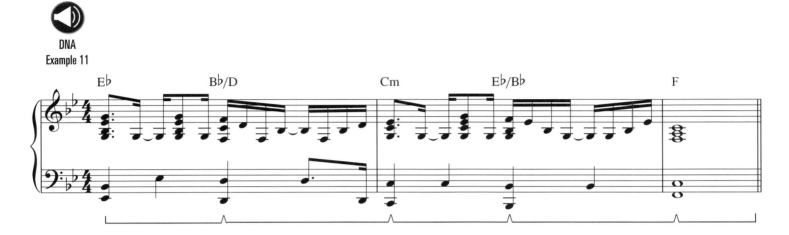

DNA
Example 11

This example has the 16th-note rhythmic subdivision and feel that is a characteristic of Elton's pop ballads. Here, the main purpose of the left-hand thumb subdivisions is to add extra momentum on the backbeats (i.e., beats 2 and 4 of each measure).

For example, in the first measure the left hand plays the root-5th (E♭ and B♭) on beat 1, which will continue to sound during beat 2, assuming that the sustain pedal is used. On beat 2, the left hand thumb adds the root (E♭) an octave higher. Similarly, the bass note of the B♭/D chord (D) is restruck by the thumb on beat 4.

The left hand pinky is also adding a 16th-note pickup into beat 1 of the second measure; see Techniques Examples 7–9.

Meanwhile, the right hand is using various staple Elton John techniques:
- Octave-doubled triads on the E♭ and Cm chords, including on the second 16th of beat 2; landing on this weak 16th creates a dynamic syncopation here
- 9th-to-3rd resolution on the B♭/D chord, and 9th-to-root resolution on the E♭/B♭ chord
- Single-note anticipations of beats 2 and 4 in each measure

Finally, for this left-hand thumb subdivisions technique, we have a two-measure example in the style of Elton's classic Intro and Interlude on "Your Song":

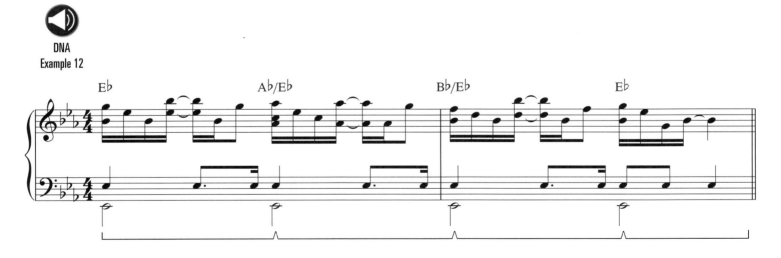

DNA
Example 12

This ballad example again has a 16th-note feel, this time with more right-hand arpeggios used during beats 1 and 3 in each measure. Here, the left-hand thumb is not only playing on the backbeats, but also adding 16th-note pickups into beat 3 of each measure.

For example, at the start of the first measure, the left-hand pinky plays and holds the E♭ for two beats. An octave above, the left-hand thumb also plays the E♭ on beat 1, then also on beat 2, and on the last 16th of beat 2 (picking up into beat 3).

Above this left-hand part, the right hand is playing 16th-note arpeggios and two-note intervals, again anticipating beats 2 and 4 in each measure.

Each two-beat phrase in the right hand is most conveniently played within an octave-doubled triad hand position. For example, on the first E♭ major chord, the right-hand thumb and pinky should be on the lower and higher B♭, respectively. Then the two-note intervals (B♭–G and E♭–B♭) and the individual arpeggio tones of the E♭ major triad are all conveniently accessible. Similarly, for the next A♭/E♭ chord, the right-hand thumb and pinky should be on the lower and higher A♭, respectively – and so on.

Chord inversions in the bass

Here "chord inversions in the bass" refers to the technique of placing a chord over its 3rd or 5th (or occasionally, 7th) in the bass voice, or lowest note played in the left hand. This is a harmonic technique that Elton John uses to great effect in his writing and playing. Most often the upper chord will be a major or minor triad, although sometimes Elton will invert basic four-part chords (i.e., major 7ths, minor 7ths, or dominant 7ths) in this way.

The use of the word "inversion" in this context may be different to how you have used this term up to now. Note that we are not talking here about different inversions of chords played in the right hand, which are chosen for voice leading and register reasons, as we have seen in the examples throughout this this book. Rather, we are talking about "inverting" a chord over its own 3rd, or over its own 5th, in the bass voice (instead of playing the root of the chord in the bass).

This harmonic technique is often used to help create a smooth, melodic bass line between consecutive chords, as we will see in the following example. This is written in the style of Elton's comping on "Goodbye Yellow Brick Road":

DNA
Example 13

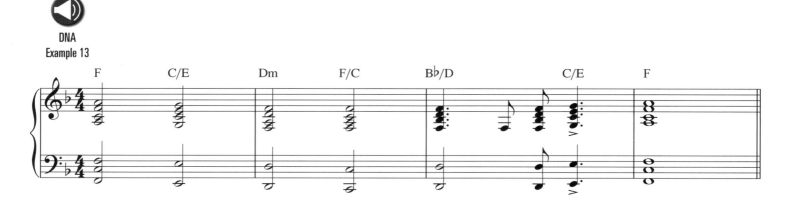

This simple comping pattern uses half-note and whole-note voicings, with some extra subdivisions in the third measure, leading to a strong accent halfway through beat 3. Note the specific use of inversions in the bass in this example:

- In the first and third measures, the C/E chord is a C major triad placed over its 3rd (E) in the bass.
- In the second measure, the F/C chord is an F major triad placed over its 5th (C) in the bass.
- In the third measure, the B♭/D chord is a B♭ major triad placed over its 3rd (D) in the bass.

Together with the other chords used, these inversions create a descending stepwise bass line (F, E, D, and C) in the first two measures. This type of melodic bass movement is found in numerous Elton John songs. Also in this example, a big sound is created by the combination of the right-hand octave-doubled triads with the left-hand roots played in octaves.

Next we have a six-measure example, written in the style of Elton's comping on the verse of "Little Jeannie":

DNA
Example 14

This example has a busier rhythmic feel than the last example, with more eighth-note subdivisions and anticipations. The right-hand triads (some with octave doubling) land on beat 1 of each measure, followed by individual arpeggio tones on upbeats later in the measure. The left hand plays a simple octave pattern, landing on beats 1 and 4, and either anticipating or landing on beat 3. All this creates a gentle series of syncopations that builds momentum within the comping pattern.

In this example, the use of inversions in the bass again results in a stepwise bass line. We can analyze these inversions as follows:
- In the first measure, the Ab/Eb chord is an Ab major triad placed over its 5th (Eb) in the bass. (As this moves to the following Eb major chord, we hear a backcycle or IV–I movement in Eb; see Stylistic DNA Examples 1–3.)
- In the third measure, the Bb/F chord is a Bb major triad placed over its 5th (F) in the bass.
- In the fourth measure, the C/G chord is a C major triad placed over its 5th (G) in the bass.
- In the fifth measure, the F/A chord is an F major triad placed over its 3rd (A) in the bass.

This results in an ascending bass line (Eb, F, G, A) through this section, before the final two chords of G minor and F major.

Finally, for this chord inversions in the bass technique, we have a four-measure example in the style of Elton's forceful comping on the verse of "Someone Saved My Life Tonight":

DNA
Example 15

This ballad example again has an eighth-note feel, with the right hand playing strong octave-doubled triad voicings on all the downbeats. Supporting this, the left hand is playing the bass line in octaves on beats 1 and 3, with some eighth-note pickups added in the first and third measures.

As in Example 13, a descending stepwise bass line is created, with a series of chord inversions in the bass. One exception to this is the Db/Eb voicing in the first measure, which creates an Eb9sus (Eb suspended dominant) chord: here the Db triad is built from the 7th of the overall Eb9sus chord, not inverted over its own 3rd or 5th like the other chords.

As before, we can analyze the chord inversions used in this example:
- In the first measure, the Ab/Eb chord is an Ab major triad placed over its 5th (Eb) in the bass.
- In the second measure, the Ab/C chord is an Ab major triad placed over its 3rd (C) in the bass, and the Gb/Bb chord is a Gb major triad placed over its 3rd (Bb) in the bass.
- In the third measure, the Db/Ab chord is a Db major triad placed over its 5th (Ab) in the bass, and the Eb/G chord is an Eb major triad placed over its 3rd (G) in the bass.

Again, these inversions help create the smooth bass-line movement that many Elton John songs are noted for.

MUST HEAR

Elton John has had a long and successful career, recording over 30 studio albums, as well as various compilations, soundtrack albums, and live recordings. Here are 20 of Elton's essential studio albums that you should check out.

Elton John, 1970
Essential Tracks
Your Song
Take Me to the Pilot
Border Song

Tumbleweed Connection, 1970
Essential Tracks
Amoreena
Burn Down the Mission

Madman Across the Water, 1971
Essential Tracks
Tiny Dancer
Levon
Indian Sunset

Honky Chateau, 1972
Essential Tracks
Honky Cat
Rocket Man
Mona Lisas and Mad Hatters

Don't Shoot Me I'm Only the Piano Player, 1973
Essential Tracks
Daniel
Have Mercy on the Criminal
Crocodile Rock

Goodbye Yellow Brick Road, 1973
Essential Tracks
Funeral for a Friend/Love Lies Bleeding
Candle in the Wind
Bennie and the Jets
Goodbye Yellow Brick Road
Saturday Night's Alright for Fighting

Caribou, 1974

Essential Tracks
The Bitch Is Back
Don't Let the Sun Go Down on Me

Captain Fantastic and the Brown Dirt Cowboy, 1975

Essential Tracks
Tower of Babel
Someone Saved My Life Tonight

Blue Moves, 1976

Essential Tracks
Sorry Seems to Be the Hardest Word
Bite Your Lip (Get Up and Dance)

A Single Man, 1978

Essential Tracks
It Ain't Gonna Be Easy
Song for Guy

21 at 33, 1980

Essential Tracks
Little Jeannie
Sartorial Eloquence

Jump Up!, 1982

Essential Tracks
Blue Eyes
Empty Garden (Hey Hey Johnny)

Too Low for Zero, 1983
Essential Tacks
I'm Still Standing
I Guess That's Why They Call It the Blues

Ice on Fire, 1985
Essential Tracks
This Town
Nikita

Sleeping With the Past, 1989
Essential Tracks
Healing Hands
Sacrifice

The One, 1992
Essential Tracks
Simple Life
The One

Duets, 1993
Essential Tracks
Don't Let the Sun Go Down on Me
Don't Go Breaking My Heart

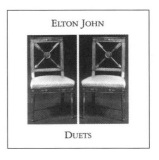

Made in England, 1995
Essential Tracks
Believe
Made in England

PLAY LIKE ELTON JOHN

Songs from the West Coast, 2001

Essential Tracks
I Want Love
This Train Don't Stop There Anymore

The Union (with Leon Russell), 2010

Essential Tracks
Eight Hundred Dollar Shoes
Hey Ahab
Never Too Old

MUST SEE

Seeing these Elton John video performances will give you some great insights into his unique playing style. Check out as many of these as you can!

On DVD / Blu-Ray

The Million Dollar Piano, 2014

Classic Elton John performances from his residency at Caesar's Palace in Las Vegas. Remarkable concert footage as well as spectacular visual effects.

Elton 60: Live at Madison Square Garden, 2007

From Elton's 60th birthday sellout performance at Madison Square Garden, recorded on March 25th, 2007.

Classic Albums: Elton John – Goodbye Yellow Brick Road, 2001

Outstanding interviews of Elton John, producer Gus Dudgeon, lyricist Bernie Taupin, and Elton's band members discussing the writing and recording process for this classic album.

Elton John: Live in Barcelona, 1992

Terrific concert footage that captures the hectic energy of Elton's 1992 world tour, in support of his album *The One*.

Elton John: To Russia with Elton, 1979

A vintage Elton John performance with percussionist Ray Cooper. Elton was the first Western rock star invited to perform in Russia.

Biography: Elton John, 2008

Behind-the-scenes footage of Elton preparing for his show at Caesar's Palace in Las Vegas. Includes music, performances, home videos, and more.

Elton John: The Red Piano, 2009

Superb music and showmanship from Elton's "Red Piano" show on the Las Vegas strip during the mid-2000s.

On YouTube

Use the following search terms to find these essential Elton John video performances.

Elton John – 2002 – London – The Royal Opera House

A wonderful Elton John performance with a choir and full orchestra, plus interviews of Elton with the band and orchestra members.

Elton John at the Staples Center – 2014

Video of Elton playing the last show of his 2014 North American tour, at the Staples Center in Los Angeles.

Elton John – 2001 – Ephesus – The Great Amphitheatre

Elton playing solo (just piano and vocal) in a beautiful amphitheater setting in Ephesus, Turkey.

Elton John – Live at Festival De Vina 2013

A glorious, high-energy performance at the Festival De Vina in Chile.

Elton John performs "Benny and the Jets" on *Soul Train* – 1975

Classic archive footage of Elton performing "Benny and the Jets." Check out the green outfit!

Elton John – "Crocodile Rock" Live at the Queen's Diamond Jubilee

Elton performing at the Queen's Diamond Jubilee concert, near Buckingham Palace in London; June 4, 2012.

Elton John – 2014 – Manchester – Bonnaroo Festival

Elton in fine form at this full concert recording of his performance at the Bonnaroo festival in Manchester, U.K.